Poetry from the Balkans

Edited

by

Fahredin Shehu

inner child press international, ltd.

Credits

Author
The Balkan Poets

Editor
Fahredin B. Shehu

Cover Design
Inner Child Press International

Quotes
Fahredin B. Shehu

Project Manager
Fahredin B. Shehu

General Information

Poetry from the Balkans

The Balkan Poets

1st Edition: 2018

This Publishing is protected under the Copyright Law as a "Collection". All rights for all submissions are retained by the individual author and or artist. No part of this publishing may be reproduced, transferred in any manner without the prior **WRITTEN CONSENT** of the "Material Owner" or its representative, Inner Child Press. Any such violation infringes upon the Creative and Intellectual Property of the Owner pursuant to International and Federal Copyright Law. Any queries pertaining to this "Collection" should be addressed to the Publisher of Record.

Publisher Information

Inner Child Press:

intouch@innerchildpress.com
www.innerchildpress.com

This Collection is protected under U.S. and International Copyright Laws.

Copyright © 2018: William S. Peters Sr.

ISBN-13:978-1970020595 (inner child press, ltd.)
ISBN-10:1970020598

$ 27.95

On the mirror of my being
let me show you the sparkling beauty
of your Soul

Dedication

This extraordinary book is dedicated to the all those who still believe in the Miracle of Unity of Mankind

When you enter in the Hell
close the gate from the inside

Table of Contents

Foreword ix

Poetry from the Balkans 1

Albania	3
Bosnia	27
Bulgaria	41
Croatia	59
Cyprus	69
Greece	95
Hungary	105
Montenegro	115
Romania	135

Table of Contents... *continued*

Kosovo	155
Macedonia	181
Serbia	205
Slovenia	239
Turkey	263

Foreword

There is no the best Poetry Anthology ever, nor it will ever be done. For I happen to realize that Poetry is beyond collective liking and subjective purpose for unifying all which is impossible and what we may consider outstanding it is just a mere ephemeral enthusiasm and/ or temporary thrill. The truth is that the Poets represented in this Anthology are more than that. More than people who represent a written word of respective Countries. They are their best ambassadors of Culture, Art, Humanity and Civilization which goes Global.

In about 300 pages the reader is invited to immerse in a splendor of a written word by a living Masters of contemporary Balkan Poetry. This will indeed trigger attention, obey the thirst for knowing other nations and their artistic legacy, build bridges of understanding of the other and much more.

The attention has been paid to create balance of different generation so we have young middle age and crafted masters of modern Balkan poetry as well as gender balance so we have a palette of genuine Poets and Poetesses to be offering in English their art for wider audience.

I am privileged to hardly work on connecting people, gathering their material, mixing with their souls from whom I have learned many new things and I hope the reader will have too, the pleasure of getting to know more about Modern Poetry in this part of Europe.

It was my original aim to bring forth these voices and diffuse them into wider readership and the Miracle here lays to reflect and respond to the pulsating impulse of creativity which is indeed a driving force of every Artist shown here in its best element.

I am extremely grateful to the Publishers who released all ties to my hands, so I was free to invite Poets aiming to select among the best.

Grateful too to all Poets participating and trusting in my efforts to accomplish this task.

fahredin b. shehu

Kosovo

Poetry

from the

Balkans

Bigger the silence bigger the hearing
bigger the hearing, bigger the knowing

Albania

Poetry from the Balkans

Olimbi VELAJ (1971) was born in Mallakastra, Albania. She studied in Tirana and Sofia. Velaj is author of the lyric volumes *Çastet vdesin nën akrepa orësh* (*Moments perish under the hands of clocks*), Tirana, 1998; and *Qenia pasdite* (*Afternoon existence*), bilingual volume (Albanian-English, Tirana, 2003. Her poetry is published in 15 languages, in Balkan countries, in Europe and Azia in some of literature magazines and anthology. She has been in a number of poetry festivals and she has nominations and awards for her poetry. Velaj translates into Albanian contemporary poets.

Velaj works as a lecturer in Albanian Literature of XX century, Creative Writing and World Literature of the Nineteenth Century; she is Head of Literature Department, Faculty of Education "Aleksandër Moisiu" University, Durrës, Albania. Currently she is teaching Albanian Language, Literature and Culture in University of Belgrade, Department of Albanology.

Velaj worked as a journalist in cultural issues from 1993 till 2008 and she was one of representative journalist during transition, after communist regime in Albania. As a journalist she has published widely in cultural heritage and folklore. During 1997-1998 she had a research fellowship in Sofia University, focused on comparative studies on Ballads of the Balkans. Her PhD topic (2012) was "The Albanian ballad in the inter-Balkan context". Her research interests are in areas of oral based literature and poetry, ballad theory and folk songs.

MOOD

You still want to dive
To the bottom of thirst and misunderstanding
Beyond all afternoons and moods
That lost their eyes in secret deliriums
You still want to speak of your mother
Filled with secrets exploding
Beyond her milk
Withered is your walk
Side by side with sounds and me
Your body
Falling through air
With its fragile bones
Thrust into dreams
You still get lost
Like the meaning of tiredness
Over a place
Where innocent bodies steal away
And burn without the time
Measuring
Our irreversible wane

THE TIME OF BELLS

We hope yet
Here comes the time of bells
With the dead sighing
Under black suits
And dry flowers
Air tightens under the silent weight
Of anxiety in the church yard
Surrounded with smelling paraffin
Angels wandering on the walls
According to faith and desire
Time takes another shape
Under tired faces of saints
And rumbling psalms
I would like to die
In one of these days
Without my atheism
Or the distant erotic
Reaching the sky
Before prayers and candles

OLD TIMES

You too remember
Those old times
With naïve calls and postcards
Summer, like an apocalypse, had flown away
Over our bodies and dreams
Waiting, overwhelmed with anxiety
As embassies creaked under screams
I cannot forget your conviction
And the pure light
Under that sky of departure hours…
Then rains came back
Our longing grew distant
And anxiety kept fading
Like an ice cube with melted corners
Senses experienced other moods
And impressions became vague
Like thirst going out of attention
Now I remember you quite accidentally,
Unconsciously, as if you were a participant
In a ritual anniversary where reason cannot work

English translation by Ukë Zenel Buçpapaj

Ervin Hatibi (b. 1974) was born in Tirana and studied French at the Foreign Language Institute there. He managed to publish a first volume of poetry during the dictatorship, but it was during the 1990s that his unconventional verse became popular, in particular with students in Tirana and elsewhere.

Among his verse collections are: **Përditë shoh qiellin** (I watch the sky every day), Tirana 1989; **Poezi** (Poetry), Tirana 1995; **Pasqyra e lëndës** (Table of contents), Tirana 2004. He is also the author of essays, notably **Republick of Albanania**, Tirana 2005. Hatibi is also a figurative artist who has exhibited his works both in Albania and abroad.

They'll Invent a Substance or a Machine

Soon they'll invent a substance
Or a machine, who knows, women will succeed,
And men will, too,
In slimming magically, "butterflies of some tragic drink
That go blind inside the chalice of youth,"
In losing weight, their exact dimensions will scorn us.
The sweat of the architect physician will drip, like a compass,
On that boiled rose,
That bourgeois French revolution
Which divides the bum from the back - the panting of the girl
Whom I loved, eleven-years-old she was.
In short, the erotic erosion of fat will appear in the headlines
The tests, the reactions,
Extremely precise, no trauma, the slimming machines
In clinics will exorcize all that fellow's culinary excesses,
His belly filled with savings for a subscription or a yoga course,
And the lady, sighing, will melt her rigid breasts
And will yet return with regret to the machine,
Perhaps to put on or to lose a few more pounds,
At the same time, she will firm the calves of her weary legs.
The world will be filled with the delicate creations of Rodin,
Which do it quickly, their copulating cocks like the talons of sparrows
On the high-voltage wires.
Then, they say that other machine will be invented,
That other substances which, buried in bright-coloured phials
From the slimming labs,
Will carry off the daily
Surplus
Of fat,
Cart it down to the Third World,
To the Somalis with ribs protruding from deep beneath the earth,
And inject it into their black skins, to the arid beating of drums
Under the palm trees,
All the bums and thighs and protein-filled throats,

Bequeathed on boring Swedish afternoons in Europe,
And thus all races will become brothers and equals
And all men will be happy tattoos.
(1994)

*[**Do të shpiket një lëngë ose makinë**, from the volume **Poezi**, Tirana 1995, p. 40-41.
Translated from the Albanian by Robert Elsie]*

Especially in August

At the beach: the sea!
Since we did not have a revolution,
Let's swim full of anger, deeper and deeper,
The farther from land, the closer to heaven,
Sea gulls paid on postcards, estranged from us,
Remain
On our backs,
Or rarely even unpaid remain,
Especially now in August,
We are all a deeply tanned people,
Made of native colonists,
Half nude, wrapped in rags of portentous colours,
We run down the beach, buying up baubles and watches,
We flirt and do crazy things,
Then in the shade we pray prostrated to the sun
And baptize ourselves in the faecal sea water
(the hairy faeces of women like dark-coloured crabs,
Millipede priests, bind us to these pagan rites).
Day after day come trains and wagons filled with young
Internees.
Those who wanted to have a Revolution
Or make some grimace in public,
Beaten by the traffic police all year round,
Their journey ends at the sea.
Here they are brought to chill out, correct their ways.
(a calming full of ardour, full of shouting thighs, motor boots
Of pumice, icy like quotations),
Only the sand is limp, wears you down, reminds us
Of the expulsion
From our homes
Or from the promised land,
But we chose the beach ourselves,
Jews disrobed, in underwear
Under a crematorium sun
Which capital freed from the ozone chains,
We rape one another reciprocally for nothing
As soon as we remove our textile masks, which as I said,

Enclose other humanities beneath.
As soon as summer comes,
The temperatures rise,
Democracy will reign over the abandoned city
Under the weary coups d'état of tourism.
(1994)

Sidomos në gusht*, from the volume **Poezi**, Tirana 1995, p. 58. Translated from the Albanian by Robert Elsie]*

Once Again on the Price of Bananas

Bananas from Rome once grew menacingly
Behind the Berlin Wall,
The year nineteen eighty something,
Jungles of concrete and steel and panic,
Men were wolves or monks for one another, surrounded
By bananas
On an island encircled
By sparkling red water,
Ich bin ein Berliner,
But in fact, I'm an American Czech who...
Post-Marxism still evolutionist reproduced
Black bananas made of rubber
For post-
Stalinists, the grandsons of dervishes, to beat
Our people with (**end of quotation**),
Bananaland stuffed with fried sweet potatoes,
The potato is still food, underground sustenance
Sown on the museum fields of Mauthausen, Treblinka.
With potatoes we make chips, with the other hand
In the dark we caress
The tepid belly of the television set, full of Coca Cola,
Chips, not potatoes, are related to bananas,
Chips and bananas and the Coca Cola, too,
All related by marriage
And dowry to Madonna
And first gave birth to dead
Bananas from Rome
Now manufactured together
In the same clump
With black rubber cudgels.

*Edhe një herë mbi çmimin e bananeve, from the volume **Pasqyra e lëndës**, Tirana 2004, p. 37. Translated from the Albanian by Robert Elsie*

Gazmend Krasniqi was born in Shkodra and lives in Tirana (Albania). He is a writer, essayist, anthologist and literary historian; Krasniqi's poems have been published in several anthologies of poetry, in English (New European Poets – USA); English, French, German (www.transcript-review.org); Poésie Albanese (Belgium); Italian; Hungarian, Serbian-Croatian etc. Among his publications are poetry volumes, prose works, plays and studies about the Albanian poetry.

AGORA

When baby kicks of light on glass,
That announces the morning's arrival, become
Increasingly tedious, when the girl's toys, here and there
In the room, make noise even more than
the breaking daily news, it reminds me
that I touched in a dream the idea
of the pure being- an instant after midnight, after all books
are read, all movies are watched, after all shoes
are worn out, in all virtual landscapes of TV-s
Could I still be the king of the universe?
I ask, since I am, the river of matter flows through the fingers,
Since the discourse of gambling destiny bills occurs
and vetoes the affluence of their vocabulary,
as large as the stalls of cheeseparing
in the middle of the square, where I pass through every day.
In moments when the body would feel strong enough as the words
– the rare, fragile, treacherous ones – I had
hoped to talk for long also about love,
so fast, so humane, as austere as
one says to death: "Good morning, dear !",
but the fate day doesn't come: when the sun trumpet opens
in unpleasant forms, that maybe on the pure being is
able to save, is it worth doing philosophy, I can
Socrates in my head saying: "so many things I don't need
are here", only that what fulminates time and again –
in my bag, it's not a meteorite of words, but pure Greek salt.

THE CHAIR

When talking in the family about old furniture,
The chair dreams of a volcano.
In wakefulness it might like the baroque, they are
fashionable even the abrupt, the rugged and drama.
When it supposes I am Plato, it goes slightly awry:
perhaps in its memory. Number One strikes
to the wall of my senses, where I put the shoulder,
when it awaits a poem of glory, or to prevail
Justice and the Good, be it in the shape of the box
or a circle, or seek to manage to escape from
this bag of Beauty–a book widely opened
for the closed eyes. Probably Books of Knowledge
will grow up in it. Probably it reads to me
that everyone is born with its own wood, the Pinocchio
of dazes, which waits to be taken by hand from the Faerie
that gets tired of old furniture.

AT PARENT'S HOME

In playful light branches, new
Parrots say old words: I know
The bizarre whistles
Asking for the instant astonishment.
Lambency coming out of copybook dust,
throughout the home spider thread,
would it reveal the great dreams
of childish verses? I push doors
The same as the tired shadows in hearts –
I come to say that the End is the Beginning.
Something similar to poetry:
wall – door; wall –door; wall – door.
I would like to be he who you wanted
me to be, but it is late for any return.
From evening to dawn, if you keep
Me again away from your invisible world,
That door bearing the word "God",
or "Eternity", the whole memory
can be the evidence of the attempt
if darkness is written by light,
If I would give a voice or fate,
If I am imprisoned or
in good company. That star
that brightens in the darkness layers,
It's not the nostalgia of something:
I smoked the life cigarette,
Where are you visions, words, gestures
bearing the insistence of predecessor's assumptions

Translated by: Granit Zela

Poetry from the Balkans

Agron Tufa was born in 1967 in Diber, Albania. He studied Albanian philology at the University of Tirana and later world literature at the Maxim Gorky Literature Institute in Moscow. There he also studied at the Russian State University for the Humanities (RGGU), where he obtained his MA in literary translation, with emphasis on the poetry of Joseph Brodsky. He is a poet, author, translator from Russian and a 20th Century Foreign Literature professor at the Philological Faculty at the University of Tirana. His works include the books of poetry *Aty tek portat Skee* (There at the Scaean Gates, 1996), *Rrethinat e Atlantidës* (The Surroundings of Atlantis, 2002), *Avangardë engjëjsh* (Vanguard of Angels, 2005), *Fryma mbi ujëra* (Spirit upon waters, 2007), *Gjurma në rrjedhë* (Footprint along the stream 2010) *Fragmentet e Gjësë (Fragments of It) 2012*, *Kafsha apo fantazma (The animal or the ghost) 2016* the novels *Dueli* (The Duel, 1998), *Fabula Rasa* (2004) for which he won the National Albanian "Silver Quill" Literary Award; *Mërkuna e Zezë* (Black Wednesday, 2006) and *Tenxherja* (The Pot, 2009) for which he won the National Kosovar "Rexhai Surroi" Award for the best Albanian novel; *Gurit të varrit ia rrëfej* (I confess it to the tombstone) 2015, as well as the collection of essays *Janusi qindfytyrësh* (Hundred-faced Janus, 2004) *Kuja e Mnemozinës* (Mnemozine's Howl, 2010) *Nga hiri i të vdekurve (*From the ashesof the dead), 2009, and the monographic work *Dibra me sytë e të huajve* (Dibra as foreigners have seen it, 2008). Other books by the authors: miniatures *Thembra e Akcilit* (Everyone's tendon), 2009 and short stories collection *Hyrje në psikanalizën e fshatit tonë (*Introduction to our village's psychoanalysis), to be published in 2018. He is professor of foreign literature of the XX-th century (Tirana University).

Actually, he is Executive Director of the Institute of the Studies of Communism's Crimes and Consequences.

Elegy on light

The light breaks free: each of its rays
Shatters and dies like a crystal flute upon the rocks
Where the unknown swells in its own ink.

Like kneaded dough risen from a dark wooden bowl,
Light pours forth.

Moist is the soil, overcast - the sky,
Along the brook, lie indistinct heads of soldiers
Tangled with the roots of roses.

Water long gone dry
gurgles now in a rave of guesses.

And the light breaks free,
Spills out -
A golden sack of hay
From the tiny barn window.

In my mind I run and touch,
I run and touch,
kissing with painted lips,
the bell at dawn.

Half-sobbing, I pray:
"Praise be to God for the light
Given unto us, greater than the Illuminator!"

Wave after wave, wave after wave,
Licking like the body of Aphrodite,
Sweeping the darkness
Until the light grabs hold the summits.

English versions by Elvana Zaimi & Craig Czury

Angels in Crisis

… I had just returned from the last war. My hands were longing for the plough as I headed for the shed. I pushed open the door and, when I got used to the dark and the damp that reeked of mould and mildew, I was overcome by the vision before me – a bale of angels sneezing in the corner. One had swollen glands and couldn't swallow, another gasped and struggled for breath. The other anemic angels stammered in low voices to explain that one of their number had fallen tragically in love with the curved blade of the coarse-toothed saw on the other wall, but it had shown no interest in him. The third angel was all in a flutter trying desperately to say something, but failed because a fourth angel was squeezing his esophagus for fun as the poor fellow gaped and belched for a full two to three minutes. A sorry sight they were indeed, sallow and covered in fungus, all huddled in a corner with less space than the sheaves of rye. I poked at them with my pitchfork and threw them out into the sun. Then, telling the farm hand to give them a cup of hot tea and some biscuits, I cautiously inquired if they could remember the goal of their forgotten mission.

English version by Robert Elsie

The Old House

1.
The roof tiles are gone from the old house. This is how the mystery faded…
Posts and rafters stand naked, busted – the entire decrepit structure of the roof;
Now it resembles an ancient ship tossed in the storm out to shore
stamped eternally on the gravure of a bad reverie. Careful, don't move
a sliver, not one beam stained black from smoke and the soot of years,
until a flash of lightning strike and preserve the breath of rituals in the skies –
the salt of childhood dreams, sorrows, curses, the unsuppressed tears
that clothed this haven with longing. Before the house is deserted
like Noah's arc upon new shores, feel the blossoming hope
and the stone-cold heart that pierces like the arrow of a fugitive mind.

2.
The sand. Its grainy structure: black and white.
The house sinks a little each day,
until the sea rises from the deep in waves and storm
to uncover it again, posts, rafters and all.

Perhaps the wanderer will return to spend the night
in a roofless shelter… a lonely traveler here
will have incoherent, disconnected dreams
of our childhood hungers – ambitions and sin.

Perhaps the mountain birds, like ghosts
will avoid the storm, chirplessly.
Perhaps UFOs will raise their studios on this very threshold
renewing their earth-sky signals.

In that case, the abstract plasma
of our dreams will return in images of desire…
Defeated and confused, within a night
the cosmic tenants will leave. One way or another…

The sand. Its grainy structure: black and white.
The frottage drawing will never fade.
And if imagination colors shadows, this house
will eternally pulsate memories, like a gravure.

3.
Like bold quotation marks over roof tiles, the cats, stretching;
gardens lush with sweet, moist nectar.
The ivy spreads – a fast notebook drawing
gulping down the corner walls of the house.
The old desolate awning. The emerald window arches sweat
like the foreheads of the dead. Nothing but cold dew on the doorframe…
The void pupils of the windows, like amber spheres
our once-eyes sealed within – forever trapped –
puzzled gazes – hostages, embalmed.
The trellis' leafy weavings like a flight of swallows
hide those gazes from me… leave me in a dilemma,
uncertain as to which gaze is my own...

English version by Ani Gjika

Albania

Nikollë Loka ka lindur në Mirditë më 25 mars 1960.
Nikolla herët ka shkruar poezi dhe gazetari. Në vitin 1988 ai ishte fituesi i çmimit të dytë në publicitet të dhënë nga gazeta "Zëri i Rinisë". Ai është autor i pesë vëllimeve poetike:
"Njerëzit që plaken në udhëkryqe", 1998;
"Kohë e shkelur" 1999;
"Larg nga Atdheu", 2001;
"Harku i Ylberit", 2013;
"Heren Tjeter " 2015.
Pjesëmarrës në shumë antologji poetike brenda dhe jashtë vendit. Fitues i shumë çmimeve kombëtare në konkurset letrare. Çmimi i dytë në "Premio literario-Terre Lontane, edicioni III" në Itali, 2016. Anëtar i Jurisë në shumë gara letrare në hapësirën Shqiptare. Anëtar i një Jurie shumë prestigjoze në Festivalin Ndërkombëtar të Poezisë "Veliero", maj 2017, në Torre Melisa të Kalabrisë në Itali.

Another time

You came to tell me that the word is windy
and doesn't have a form.
A promise is a game,
Because the human and the dog are the same.
You came to tell me
that the time oldenst you trickily,
and the wrinkles in your forehead
are put stealthily,
telling you love words.
It is bringing me words
from an abyss to another one,
that time stays tightly in your pulse.
In the ether another time is coming.
Your time with another sun,
and another moon.

I've seen in the midnight

I've seen in the midnight
the mystic sky on the ground laying.
Above it the stars got drunk with air,
and go and come on something hidden.
And thousands of butterflies completed
with colors an empty space.
I've come down seven stairs
under seven sky shadows,
where clouds crashed
in the sea shore like waves.
I've crashed with my foot my own shadow,
just when it came near me.
I crashed it without any hurt.

The magnet of the soul

A wave of your soul was burned with thirst,
and that fire made the sky blue.
I have turned into a stone
that waits the other wave,
to clean off the passion
or the passion to clean me off,
In the mirror of time
you embroider the blue,
from my stone,
violet water drops
and the blue blood
that you mention so many times,
I feel how it drips amongst seas.
That blueness set under the skin,
the heart drowns in the lake.
In seven sources
that come from the same rock
my soul mentions you.
And your sky remained
just like a cloud,
a magic of your eyes a mirror.
My magnet soul that attracts
you, your magnet
soul that only pushes me.

Translator: Laureta Rexha

Bosnia

Poetry from the Balkans

Ferida Duraković, poet, short story writer, columnist, children writer. Graduated from the University of Sarajevo, Bosnia-Herzegovina. Published 15 volumes of poetry, prose, children books and translations. Some books: *Srce tame* (Heart of Darkness), poetry, 1993: *Locus minoris – Sklonost Bosni kao melanholiji* (Locus minoris – Inclined to Bosnia as to Melancholy), poetry, 2008; *Putnici kroz (ne)vrijeme – 50 godina Sarajevskih dana poezije* (koautorstvo, 2011), (Travellers through (Bad) Times – 50 Years of the Sarajevo Poetry Days, co-author, 2011), *Pokret otpora* (Resistence), essays and columns, 2012.

Among others, awarded with Hellman-Hammet *Fund for Free Expression* in 1992, and *Vasyl Stus Freedom-to-Write Award* given by PEN New England, U.S.A. for poetry book *Heart of Darkness* (White Pine Press, Fredonia, New York, 1999). Books of poetry translated also in Italy and Bulgaria. Poems translated into 20 languages. Worked as Executive Director of PEN Center in Bosnia-Herzegovina in Sarajevo since its founding in 1992 until 2013. Lives in Sarajevo with husband, daughter, and three cats.

GEORG TRAKL ON THE BATTLEFIELD AGAIN IN 1993

Our Dear Lord dwells high above the planes, in the highest Heaven,

with His golden eyes settled on the darkness of blackened Sarajevo.

Cherry blossoms and shells are falling outside my window.

Madness and me, alone. We are alone. Alone.

translated by the author

Beauty and The Beast

An Untruthful Beauty
Slammed the door
Finally
As the Homeland did,
Then vanished
Into History.

Nonetheless, Beauty,
Untruthful one,

And the Homeland

Have something in common –
Both of them leave behind

The boys

Who will die

For them.

Translated by the author

Ten Year Old Girl Perceives Her Homeland While Watching the Ocean 1995.

    I.

This morning I took a long walk through the forest
which was made by J.R.R. Tolkien
when he was in a real good mood.
Then I sat there
on the sunlit mountain slope
looking at the Ocean
waiting for a huge whale to come up
from all that water.
But he did not show,
and I ate an apple instead.

    II.

Those (I think) who know what
I am writing about
will not need to keep on
reading these lines.
And those who do not know
what I am writing about
will start another war, back there
far, far away, in my tiny homeland
which was also made by J. R. R. Tolkien
when he was in a good mood, but

ALL OF A SUDDEN
SOMEBODY KNOCKED
AT HIS STUDY DOOR, AND

the happy ending (which he was really good at)
simply slipped off his mind.

After that he died
at the age two hundred fifty
and never finished the story...

III.

Today I am awaiting him
to come up from all that water:
somebody must give an end
to my tiny homeland story.
I do not know whether Mr. President
can do something to make him return --
he has, you know, those Striders
and all that stuff --

Anyway
I guess I will just sit here and
wait for a while.
I think I deserve it. I have been
a good girl, after all.
I am just a little bit afraid of the dark
coming from far away
across the Ocean.

Otis, Oregon, February 1995

P.S.
This is my first poem written in English. I wrote it a couple of months before the war in Bosnia was over thanks to Mr. President of the U.S.A. So, anyone can see that poetry is a matter of magic.

Naida Mujkić (1984) is a Bosnian poetess. She won first prize at literary festival *Slovo Gorčina* – the most important award to young poet in the collection of unpublished poems in her country (2006). She was a guest artist at Q21 Museumsquartier Wien (Austria, 2016.) and Goten Publishing (Macedonia, 2017.).
Books of poetry:
Oscilacije, Zoro, Sarajevo-Zagreb, 2008. *Ljubavni šarti mogula*, Buybook, Sarajevo-Zagreb, 2015. *Šafran, CKO*, Tešanj, 2016.
Bašta ne cvjeta, CKO, Tešanj, 2017. Book of lyrical prose: *Kad sam padala u travu,* CKO, Tešanj, 2017.
So far, her poems have appeared in many places in the world, as well as in some of the influentual magazines (such as: *Lichtungen, Poezija, Izraz, Razlika/ Differance, Behar, BKG...*). Her poems are elected in the Anthologies of contemporary bosnian poetry, as well as in the anthologie of Balkan's youngest generation of poets. She participated in several international poetry festivals.

Purification

Under black dog tags they came from Ogrozdon, everyone of them
Was the eyewitness of the one next to it, in tangled bones
Of last year's falls. Niggardly, tinned in its own
Dusky question. – Well, where are you? it asked me
While rolling easier then the moon.
- Inside of you – I answered. But black nuts didnt hear me.
Then I felt checkered napkin with skulls on it, over it
My mother lived a life as if it was her own.
No one noticed our secret moral.
Our steps into emptiness.
Power not to say: We are the criminals that soak the witnesses
Into ourselves, and for that we are ineffably grateful.
Our heart closed in masks died thousand times since then
In front of outer walls in which we felt breath of old age.
Even before we learned that we shouldn't go far
To forget chords of the apocalypse that cover our garden.
We closed the entrance door to our house. We didn't know if we should go out or not.
Downpour wasn't starting when I decided to run away from her.
I passed between daisy and edelweiss. They were protected by cobweb.
I tried not to snag them. Though edelweiss yelled: *come to me!*
I closed my eyes, terrified. Mother was still in the kitchen, same swing
With a meat hammer. Same cracking of dog tags under fingers.
She wanted to clean her body of parasites, worms and fungus.
But, she doesn't yell at them, or picks up their body liquids.
 She just bumps and bumps.
I opened my eyes, horrified.
It's the caterpillar, licking my foot.

Crucifix

I wanted to come in, but mother
pulled my sleeve which was a sign
to stay
by the invisible line, next to fallen fruit
that we used to make fig schnapps.
Father brought ten wooden sticks and halved them
With his knee. I added him every one of them
But the first one. Then, with his hands, he pressed them
Into the earth.
Moisture was absorbed by the ropes that I cut
That morning before water for the coffee got boiled.
We tied it up on all sides. Mother told us
To watch the leafage. I used
The moment, when she and father
Started to stretch it, and
Threw two into my dress.
Now, I had to be even more careful.
I fixed a ribbon around my waist. They squirm
In my navel like the sentences that I was tying
Around pegs.
  * * *
Behind accordionist in a beret, wet cigarette butts are falling down,
like barrel covers. And the sun. I turn toward the man that sits
at the next table. But, he was not that man. There were no
bags underneath his glasses. He leaned over postcards in front of me.
I was listening to his calmness. When he waved to
accordionist, I stood up. Smell of fried sugar
swallowed my shadow. But those could be
clouds. Man wanted to see the sea.
His mother sleeps at the bottom of it.
Her hair is foamy, like the blood in a spittle.
His hair is gray. He wanted to see the sea,
but people on the rocks
were sticking sticks into
the buckets with dead fish inside.
He wanted to ask them something.
Do they still crush
red onion with their heels? They turn on them

like trapeze artists around rope. Or it drops
through their palms.
I remember sweat drops, sliding
down the glasses – that he pushes
along the root of his nose. And the red petals spread
over stones
I took the stone, and not the petal
I wanted him to put that stone into his
inner pocket – to lose it
and forget this day
I remember blisters – on both
of my pinkie fingers
And that I didn't took of
my ballet shoes - what would he
do with my wounded feet. And flies
besieging banana carts,
proving, through their movements,
that every one of them is individual -
first example from the holy book.

Bosnia

Sokolović Emir was born in 1961. His works have been translated into Italian, Polish, English, French... He has been published in many anthologies and collections. He is the creator and director of the prestigious international literary festival "Pero Živodraga Živković". So far, he published:
- „Dove e perche/ Gdje i zašto" – Edizione Foreman, Bergamo 1983.
- „Apokalipsa" – intermedijalni projekat TV Zetel, 1994.
- „Una era canna allora/ Bio je tada trska" – autorsko izdanje 1998.
- „Paris – ili zalud je razapinjeti Krista" – autorsko izdanje 1999.
- „Oslobađanje" – autorsko izdanje 2003.
- „Lako je jurišati na nebo koje ćuti..." – autorsko izdanje 2011.
- „Una era canna allora" – Casa Editrice „Rocco Carabba" 2013.
- „Poetica demonica" – „Kultura snova" 2014.
- „Ples među podsjenama" – autorsko izdanje 2015.
- "Paris – ili zalud je razapinjati Krista/ Paride - È inutile crocifiggere Cristo" - „Providenca" 2015 i
- „Ogledi" – „Providenca" 2016,
- "Banka" – "Narodno pozorište RS" – 2017 i
- "Vjetrovi/ I Venti" – "Providenca" – 2017.

Babylonian Strumpet

Your Grail
was built upon your
avidity and
wantonness
You who are willing to
suffer the chastisement
due to the feebleness
of others
trusting in the righteous' shroud
speak:
 "Drink, your blood
and wine
my shame is
peerless
without my ignominy.
I am an outcast
for I wanted it to be;
I wore
crowns duly.
My Grail has been
made."

Upon Looking In The Mirror

The shame shrouded with
A tear on
The jester's
Face
Awakens holiness
On the trail and
Deadlock
Which alters
The tremor
Into laughter
Although the overshadow
Withstands
The rays
Seeking one another
And the hint of which
Was dreamy
Under the gown
To which they
Bowed
In vain…

The Healing

For the well
In his dreams
While it strides down
The score
In the form of
The drunken
Ink which
Is an excuse
To the Maestro through its
Thoughtfulness
Shows the way
Even though at
The horizon
In this hourglass
There is no grain
Nor rudder
Nor stern
Only the anchor
A knot around the neck…

Bulgaria

Kristin Dimitrova (born May 1963 in Sofia, Bulgaria) is a poet, writer and translator. Her books of poetry include *Jacob's Thirteenth Child* (1992), *A Face Under the Ice* (1997), *Closed Figures* (1998), *Faces with Twisted Tongues* (1998), *Talisman Repairs* (2001), *The People with the Lanterns* (2003), *The Cardplayer's Morning* (2008, translated into Czech) and *The Garden of Expectations and the Opposite Door* (2012). *A Visit to the Clockmaker* (2005) was published by Southword Editions, Ireland, and *My Life in Squares* (2010) by Smokestack Books, UK.

Among her works of fiction are the novel *Sabazius* (2007, translated and published in Mexico, Russia and Romania) and two short stories collections: *Love and Death under the Crooked Pear Trees* (2004), *The Secret Way of the Ink* (2010, translated into Macedonian) and *Give me a Call When You Arrive* (2017).

Dimitrova is a winner of five awards for poetry, three for fiction and two for poetry translation (John Donne and Lewis Carroll). Poems, short stories and essays by Kristin Dimitrova have been translated into 27 languages and published in 35 countries.

THREE OLD MASTERS

Christ and Saint Mary on Golgotha
by Hans Holbein the Elder (1460-1524)

They are standing close to each other
but with a gap between them
that will broaden.

She looks at him, crying for him.
He looks ahead,
crying for himself.

He sits on the cross which
so far lies on the ground.
So far.

She is all clothed, even her hair
hidden.
He is not any more.

His hands are bound in front.
His body will soon be
rendered meaningless.

The skulls of past people
are scattered about,
the sky is deep blue

for those coming after.
The painting is small and
difficult to notice.

The massacre of the innocents
by Master from Frankfurt (1460-1533?)

In the foreground a soldier,
in an exquisite silver-gray tonality,
stern but conscientious,
pierces his sword through
the tiny neck of an infant.
Looks like a geography teacher pressing
his pointer stick in some narrow isthmus
to embed it in memory.
The mother will hardly
forget the lesson.
In the background two women
have caught hold of his colleague:
one grips his hands to constrain him,
the other, clutching his throat, has raised
a clog over his head
to finish him off.
Good for you, girls.
Master from Frankfurt,
who are you, actually?

A Group of Crucifixes
by Michel Erhart (1440-45 - after 1522)

They are wooden. Naive. Scrupulously
polished and painted in human colour.
Jesus soars between the thieves
but looking none the better for it.

The three faces are twisted
into demure grimaces of horror.
The eye falls on the relatively slim
yet unathletic bodies and down below

rests on the feet.
The shins of the thieves,
in full accordance with the Gospel,
are broken,

but what a good job
they did -
the skin is torn open,
the bones sticking out.

The feet are twisted and tied
at an unnatural angle, and you almost
expect to see between knee and ankle
an extra joint.

Fifteenth century. Nobody noticed the faces.
In everything else they were experts.

Liudmila Mindova was born in 1974 in Ruse, Bulgaria. She studied Slavic philology at the Sofia University and got a Master's degree in 1998 and a PhD degree in 2006. At present she is an associate professor at the Institute for Balkan Studies & Centre of Tracology (Bulgarian Academy of Science) and a part-time lecturer at the Sofia University. In her translation are published many books by Yugoslav and post-Yugoslav authors.

She is the writer of three poetry books, two monographs on the South Slavic literatures and a novel.

In Front of the Old Master's Paintings

I had to realize that skin color
doesn't determine the color of your day,
nor the color of your dreams,
nor the color of your blood.
But must the blood start gushing
for you to see that it's blue.

Author: Liudmila Mindova
Translated from the Bulgarian by Katerina Stoykova-Klemer

How

What is the use of books?

There is no use.
It's all loss.
But what loss…

I see how the thief
returns the loot,
how the murderer
digs out the body.

(The defeated is still defeated, of course,
not to mention the deceased.)

And so
there is no use for books,
it's all loss.
But what loss –
to live with decency,
to die with honor.

Author: Liudmila Mindova
Translated from the Bulgarian by Katerina Stoykova-Klemer

Paper Boat

To A.Z.

No,
it's not the book
makes you a poet,
nor the place,
nor the time,
nor the people.
Not even the air,
But everything and nothing put together.
Because poetry is a question of breathing,

the body is a paper boat.

Translated by the author

Roman Kissiov was born in 1962 in the town of Kazanlak, Bulgaria. Poet, translator of poetry, artist. He studied at the Secondary School of Arts in his hometown and graduated in painting from the National Academy of Fine Arts in Sofia. Roman Kissiov lives and works in Sofia.

His works have been included in poetry anthologies in Bulgaria, Poland, Romania, Armenia, Serbia, Bosnia and Herzegovina, Republic of Macedonia, India, Jordan, Nagorno-Karabakh, and in the international anthology of English *POETS FOR WORLD PEACE* (Switzerland, Canada, 2011). His poems have been translated and published in 23 languages in the world.

He has taken part in many prestigious international poetry festivals.

Poetry books: *The Doors of Heaven* (1995), *The Shadow of the Flight* (2000), *Pilgrim of the Light* (2003), *Cryptus* (2004, 2007), *Voices* (2009), *The Garden of the Secrets* (2014), *Eggs of phoenix* (2014), *The Mystic Rose* (selected poems, 2016).

In other languages: *Pilgrim of the Light* (in Croatian, Croatia, 2008), *The Shepherd Word* (in Macedonian, R. of Macedonia, 2010), *Poems* (in Bengali, India, 2013), *The World of Words* (in Romanian, Romania, 2014), *Ascension* (in Armenian, Bulgarian and Russian, N.-Karabakh, 2014), *Eggs of phoenix,* e-book (in Macedonian, R. of Macedonia, 2016).

Ithaca

*"...You must have surely understood
by then what Ithacas mean"*
C. Cavafy

I am Odysseus, too,
but unknown.
No one ever heard of me,
nobody knew about my shrewdness…

Because I never left Ithaca.

Never in my life did I meet
Cyclopes, Laistrygones and Sirens.
I did not build a Trojan Horse,
I was not famous for any feats…

Because I never left Ithaca.

No one ever knew about my braveness
and the power of my bow.
Even Penelope's love for me
has long cooled down…

Because I never left Ithaca.

13. 09. 1989

The world of words

I am living in the world of words.

Everything here consists of words:
The moon and stars are shiny words.
The wind is a long angry word.
The transparent air is a silent word.
The rivers, the sea, and the sky
are vast words with many vowels.
The trees, the flowers – they're wonderful words
all abloom in the spring.
Words of passage are the birds…

I am living in the world of words.

Time is measured in words here.
Minutes are short words.
Words flow, they flow out
like grains of sand in a clepsydra.
My life is also flowing out…

But I stay on.

My life is a word
that God has spoken.
And every word of His is everlasting.

The Contemplator

I can hear the grain growing in the soil
I can hear the secrets that the sea waves
whisper to the shore
I can hear the birds' footsteps on the sand
and the crabs' footsteps on the bottom of the ocean
I can hear the groans of the condemned in hell
I can hear the cries of joy of the blessed ones in heaven

I can clearly see the embryo
in the future mother's womb
I can see the sap travelling in the tree
from its roots up to the blooming branches
And in the pupils of the children's eyes
I can see the flight of birds
I can see guardian angels
at my parents' sides

I am listening to the voice of my blood
I am staring at the shadow of my words

I am contemplating my young antiquity
And I praise the birth of my eternity

Translation from Bulgarian: Ralitsa Saramova

Ivan Hristov is a Bulgarian poet and literary researcher. He is the author of the poetry collections *Farewell, Nineteenth Century* (winner of the prize for best poetic debut from the National Southern Spring Competition 2002), *Bdin* (winner of the national literary prize Svetlostruy 2006, in 2015 *Bdin* was published in Turkey), *American poems* (2013) as well as the academic monograph *The Sagittarius Circle and the Idea of the Native* (2009). In 2016 in Romania was published the book *Bdin, followed by American poems* which contains his last two poetry books. In 2018, his fourth poetry collection called *A Dictionary of Love* came out. Since 2010, he has been a member of the organizing committee for the international Sofia: Poetics festival. He currently works at the Institute for Literature at the Bulgarian Academy of Sciences.

A
Alabaster

Alabaster is the world
In a milk-white colour
Milk-white sea
Milk-white sky
Sugar milk-white
in warm white milk
It has a porous structure
A vessel for perfumes
and essential oils
can easily be crafted

V
Vines

Exuberant greenery
brilliant hues
exterior decoration
they hide unpleasant parts
and architectural elements
Climbing
hortensia, wild grapes, ivy and tecoma
Clinging
Characteristically weak, flexible, with very long shoots
The climbing rose
Twining
known here as "the gramophone" – ipomoea
Sprawling
Asarina (lofos, maurandya)
They have the strongest decorative effect
and do the most damage
They must be strictly tended,
cut back when they get overgrown
Be careful not to let their roots take hold of your home,
The first step towards its destruction

W
Wax

The honey bee
Feeds and stings
Wax is secreted by the wax glands
in the shape of scales
as clear as glass and colorless
it turns white after mastication
growing ever yellower or brown
after the addition of pollen oils
Honeycomb
The sealing of the cells

From "A Dictionary of Love"

Translated from Bulgarian by Angela Rodel

...and I only want to rejoice my Victory in my struggle to be a humble Man only.

Croatia

IVAN HERCEG (1970), poet, prose writer and editor, was born in Krapina. He holds a BA in Croatian language and literature and South-Slavic philology from the Zagreb University. He is the executive editor of the Zagreb-based journal *Poezija*, the assistant editor of *Poezija* editions and the co-organiser of the SUR (Stih u regiji /Poetry in the Region/) Poetry Festival. He received several awards for his poetic work, most notably the *Goran* prize for young poets, the *Zdravko Pucak* prize and the *Rikard Jorgovanić* Award. His story *SMS – cvjetni porno* was featured in *Libido.hr* (Naklada MD, Zagreb, 2002), a selection of Croatian erotic stories. He also published a collection of short stories *Naked* (2011). His poetry has been widely anthologised and translated into a dozen languages. His selected poems, *Koliko Naju Bo Ostalo*, were published in Slovenian and *Warsaw, Warsaw* in Polish. Publications (poetry): *Our Other Names* (1994), *Night on Asphalt* (1996), *Photographs of Earthly Sighs* (1997), *Angels in Mourning* (2004), *Irregularities* (2007), *When Will Babylon Arrive* (2013).

Limbo

Birds fly around your legs and you count them
for eternity, but I can't figure out if you are above
or below, if you're calling me or not, or if you're just
seducing me with that barbed wire bra.
Positively, with nothing sacred in the vicinity
your walk is perfect because it's void of course.

My new eyesight is the balls of riddles.
Therein swarm decrepit days,
black dogs, candelabras and psalms.
While I am repeating incessantly:
"My other name is Limbo,
my other name is Limbo..."

Words and poems circle around your head.
I read them in a monotonous voice.
With eyes blindfolded by barbed wire:
"Violet is the devil's colour.
God is all honey and lead
and I am your mad namesake.
You remain my vulnerable jazz.
On the other side of the storm."

Dakota … The Woman Planting Soil

All of New York's secrets and malice are stored within you
and that's why I want to steal you and send you far beyond my gaze.
We will be silent protestors at Union Square,
and in Central Park we shall swirl madly and loudly
like some deadly sinners.

I will bury you close to Lennon's crossing
- just *Imagine* it – left or right, up or down.
It doesn't really matter for you are neither Christian nor Muslim.

Your breath will be your epitaph:
"Dakota – the woman planting soil"
and I will never even try to resurrect
our crumbled bodies
forever concealing the fact
that you belong to neither of the two worlds
so vicious yet vulnerable like the last living language
wherein you cannot know thyself and others
or claim a lover or a modicum of peace.

The underworld is an open home, a lovers' subway,
filled with the stink of gunpowder and urine, the final orgy
at the heart of the world, perfectly nauseating.

Sarajevo

They say that the Miljacka river does exist,
but I can only sense it in the distance.
You, on the other hand, who flow
through the night so swiftly, are real.
Your hair is black, your scarf invisible,
your hand firmly held by someone.
You're giving me that long piercing look
knowing there's so much that needs to be remembered.

In this city we are equally distant
from each other; halfway between Persia and Europe;
equally distant from all living and all dead.

I wish I could gently put out cigarettes on your arms.
I wish you would act the part of Satan for me
on the stage of some abandoned cultural centre.
Thus we would get rid of one life line,
one destiny, one string of love...
so that only those lines on my palms would remain.

How many cemeteries are there in Sarajevo?
How many in the entire world?
Does anyone ask himself.

Nobody asks that. Everybody steals the truth.
So, I'm begging you, *miraždžika,*
to please cut off my hands
with that last atom of strength.

translated by Damir Šodan

VIŠNJA GOLJAČKI is a writer, magazine editor and director of the Cultural Center from Croatia. Besides writing, she is involved in organizing cultural programs and manifestations. She is the founder of international meetings on human rights, culture and science. She has published several novels, narratives, monographs and poetry collections, and is currently preparing an English, Swedish, Spanish, Turkish and Yiddish edition of illustrated fairy tales.

Bulk Cargo

To dream awake
Dreaming the living
To look at daisies
To draw a sheep
To tame a fox
To dance with the clouds
To laugh at the wave
To wave at your friends
To water with tear
Stars that tremble
Inside you

THE TOUCH

Do not worry,
I shall come.
I shall come
On the brink
Of eyelashes
I shall reach
Near,
Near,
Almost near
To your touch.
I shall come to you
On the brink
of eyelashes
I shall be your
Tear,
Bliss,
Conciliation.
I shall come
A moment before
of an aye
before
the clapper
enters
in the storm.
I shall arrive
On the wings
Of a fallen eagle
My sail,
my high sea.
I dreamed:
I am carrying you
in the mouth,
You are in my throat
A cramp,
A scream,
A fright.
I am waking up:

Croatia

You are remoteness,
You are a lost ship,
I am a lighthouse,
I am a lost ship,
You are a lighthouse.
You are a square
In my town,
and a smoke of a chimney
in dusk
suburbs.
I shall find you.
I shall close you,
Like summer firefly
In matchbox.
And I shall watch you
In the dark.
You are glittering.
After death
I shall touch you,
I shall be
Your
unknown tomb.
My palms
Will be
Your
Requiem
My curse
Will be
Spring rain
That soothes,
And when
Your soul
Is
Oblivion
I shall not be
A cursed widow,
I shall be
A bride in white
On the brink

Of an enchanting forest
And the eyelash,
Near
Almost
Near
You.

Cyprus

Neşe Yaşın was born in 1959 in Cyprus. She is a poet well known and read on both sides of divided Cyprus. Her poem called "Which Half?" that she wrote at the age of 17 was composed by the Greek Cypriot composer Marios Tokas and became an icon of identity, an unofficial anthem for a united Cyprus.

She has published eight volumes of poetry, one novel and a research book on literature. Selections from her poetry has been translated to more than 30 languages, published in literary magazines and anthologies in different counties. A selection from her poems have been published in English translation with the title "Rose Falling Into Night". She has participated in poetry festivals and readings around the world. Among others she has received the Anthias Pierides Award in 1998.

Ode to Love

We were like the broken branches during the last looting
 deceived by the uninterrupted love-making of spring

To be one
That impossible of all desires
At the border of time

You would wake up to the verses
of your distant land
while I, a sleepy kitten
would lay in the bed of miracles

I would enter your kingdom
Through shuttered doors
with the bare feet of my fear

My mind was the wind
Talking to trees, to the clouds

My loving you
a dove taking wing
at the border of the unknown

The sudden flutter of the butterfly
The shudder of the flower

My loving you
like fireworks
Kissing the night

While fleeing in fear
She turns into a tree
makes love with the light
On a bed of Daphne leaves
You had smiled
Deep in your eyes
I saw the dream of the heart
I saw lakes, swans, shuddering branches

You had broken me
I saw lands torn apart inside me
Your raft drifting away
My own drowning
The invading galloping horsemen
You, standing on another shore

We were in the seventh night of love
In the other dimension of time
In the hidden hut of the heart
In the seclusion of the body

We were in the claws of desire
In the moisture of our tongues
At the desolation of existence
at a moment in eternity
in the eternity of moment

We returned before we reached the desired
But on our return it seemed like we had reached it

We were the fireflies of desire
the skin of the rising sea
the howling of the unknown

Remember
The city under snow
The naked bodies
The first dawn of love
The wings of innocence
The small miracle of the heart

Remember
The moans of the night
and the boats of bodies
diving in diving out

Remember the land we reached
The wet stones
Our mingling breath

Cyprus

Pulling in the thread of longing
dissolving into each other
the peace of oblivion

Remember
The shudder of the inflamed body
Our rise
The melting of wings

Remember
The desperation of desire
your forgotten serenity
drinking the magic nectar
in each other's desolation

In the silence I build up
the question burning in the void
to be strangers while close
and close while strangers
the secret melancholy of passion

What remains of you
is the street you stroll in my dreams
The steps that crush my soul
The leaf scattered in the tunnel

Remember
The last embrace
in the desert storm

If ever this poem comes flying to you
Cling onto its wings
Don't let the bittersweet memory of the heart
be orphaned

Translated by: Aydın Mehmet Ali

Variations On A Theme Of Doors

I
I wander the streets of childhood
it's the time of cruelty
hiding the dregs behind the door

II
The little girl
watches games of light
leaking through tinted windows
the whisper of life
is a shiver of the sun

III
The door's memory
is of leaving

III
My sentences cut in two
are behind the door now

IV
When you reach the city
you reach yourself
the distance within you

V
The archives of the blue dreams
of the women behind doors
are flowing towards the city

VI
The transparent silence of the night
waits before the door
like a voiceless and wounded passenger

VII
If only our door
were the same door

Cyprus

VIII
Here's this moment
wounded by the past
fearing the future
a sad door
appearing suddenly
İn front of us

IX
The city shuts its doors
thanks to inner pain

X
Behind black doors
things you don't want to know
are wounded by your presence

XI
Time
has left its weary scars
written secret sentences
on eternity

The one waiting for me
is behind which door?

XII
Why is every door
related to closing?

XIII
Open the doors
that my heart may flow

XIV
Waiting at the wind's door
was my heart's kite

XV
Morning was a door
opening to the city
the city would get up and leave

the night's embrace

XVI
Doors talk always
in time's alphabet

XVII
An angel passed through this house
dropping a feather at the door

XVIII
As the door faded
so many lives went by
shining then fading

XIX
He left and took the slam of the door with him
so that he would never return

XX
A door kept waiting
for the one who will never come

XXI
There was a woman behind the door
a rose garden inside the woman
all the roses were blooming for love

XXII
Since he left by this door
all the doors of the heart
have been moaning

Translated by Clifford Endres

Poison Apple

Once I didn't then I did exist
loneliness was my cradle
forgotten in the wind

Pearls ornamented my coverlet
evil-eye beads
frozen in stone gazed at me

When my mother loosed me from her hand
the birds lent me wings
the trees a nest

It was night
leaf on leaf the forest wept
wolves gave me their breasts

I had a step-god
He would not hear what I said

When I bit into the poison apple
my mother and my love deserted me
I was a branch crying in the frost
water drinking solitude
the voice of leaves rustling

My lover did or didn't exist
his name was the wind, his memory a fish
if I cried he did not cry
if I explained he did not understand

When I spoke I could not recognize
my voiceless voice
still one day I solved
the riddle of my wounded soul

O secret museum of my heart, open
a little girl is hiding inside

every heartbroken woman's voice
The fate of a love lost
is registered on Its bleeding country

Time is a storm that comes to rest
on broken branches
speaking deliriously of ruin

Translated by: Clifford Endres

Cyprus

Stephanos Stephanides Is a poet, essayist and memoirist, translator, ethnographer, and documentary filmmaker. He is married and has one daughter. He was born in Trikomo, Cyprus and was taken to the UK by his father when he was eight. He completed his PhD at Cardiff University, and during his student years he lived intermittently for three years in Spain, Portugal and Greece. He spent six years teaching literature at the University of Guyana, where he developed a deep interest in Caribbean Creole and Indian diasporic communities, and thereafter a lifelong engagement with India. He lived in Washington DC for seven years, before returning to Cyprus in 1992 as part of the founding faculty of the University of Cyprus. He retired as Professor of English and Comparative Literature until 2017.

Selections of his poetry have been published in more than twelve languages. He writes in English but other languages reverberate in his work. He has held residential writing and research fellowships at the University of Warwick's Centre for Translation and Comparative Cultural Studies; the Bogliasco Foundation, Italy; JNIAS at JNU, India; and Rhodes Centre for Writers and Translators, Greece. He is a writing fellow of the International Writers Program of the University of Iowa. He was awarded first prize for poetry from the American Anthropological Association, 1988, and first prize for video poetry for his film *Poets in No Man's Land* at the Nicosia International Film Festival. He was a judge for the Commonwealth Writers Prize (Eurasia Region, 2000, 2010,) is a Fellow of the English Association, and Cavaliere of the Republic of Italy. Representative publications include *Translating Kali's Feast: the Goddess in Indo-Caribbean Ritual and Fiction (*2000*), Blue Moon in Rajasthan and other poems (*2005*).*

Dwelling

Boethius — 'Nunc fluens facit tempus, nunc stans facit aeternitatum'
The now that passes produces time, the now that stays produces eternity

A rooster crows
Morning softly thumps
A medlar tree
Eagerly unburdening
Its fruit a heavy dew

Noontime hushing
A drone of disquiet
An expectancy of nectar
Only the bumblebee

Silence the watchman
Of speckled time,
With sleight of hand
Unleashes yellow butterflies

Courtyard of stony arbor
Whispers *nunc fluens nunc stans*
Rattles and squeaks
Trembling of wings
Murmuring starlings
Trace the air

Chimes of Vesper
Evening mourns
In slumbering light
Unexpectedly
A dog barks

A thousand eyes
Of sky glitter on
Cascading night
Deep in the valley
A donkey brays

Rhapsody on the Dragoman

For Susan and Harish, υψίστους διδασκάλους

Part I

I am a dragoman
courtesan of the word
I pluck my eyes to hear
with skill and improvisation
wor-l-ds of hard edges,
a treacherous and loyal
exponent of obsessions
not all men know my speech

in the night I go under
in company of dervishes and learn
why cyclamens sprout in pavement cracks
and mutter promises, amidst the dust,
of the beautiful and the unseen
I ask meaning for
fore give fore go fore play
an island warbler
still with no quarrel
or a swallow
in the line of flight
meandering with finality
knowing that the road is lost
in floating debris
of fortuitous choices
precipitous moves

with impulsive sagacity
I swirl and sail away
vexed in my state of grace
daytime dragoman
nighttime dervish

Part II
When hearts hum in the buzz
of morning light so bright it silences,
the lady arrived at the City Gate
and waited for the *tarjuman*
she had requested in a letter sent from Egypt,
someone versed in her language
to accompany her to the Sublime Porte.
Only I among the *rayahs* spoke her tongue
from that island in the northern sea.
Today, following my companion's counsel
 I shed my *kufta* and *jubbeh*,
and present myself with *boyunbagi* and waistcoat in a style
after the French.

I bow and before she presumes
to scrutinize the measure of my wisdom
If I am a fool servant or a learned scholar
I do not climb inside the carriage
I swiftly step up to the box instead and take my seat
next to the driver while I instruct the porter boy
if he receive *bakshish* to say "thank you" as her kind expect,
and reveal neither gratitude nor displeasure;
she need not know our measure of her generosity,
only count the day's profit within our own walls;
we do not know
if she desires the sweetness of the sultanina grape
or some other island sweetness.
When heaven wants to speak
 it needs few words
to open gateways here, there, and elsewhere.
Trees grow in silence
as do the date-palms lining the river
inside the city wall.

Along the path of Hermes
the wind will track the language down
as we track the dust of love
in the mausoleum smell of mourning
jasmine turning putrid.

Cyprus

When the evening drops stealthily
I will retire to the Dragoman's house
where hot stone will transform my body to vapory waters
absorbing the contours of the cypress
with long shadows of night in a crimson trance
penetrating the skylight of the hamam
yearning neither joy nor melancholy.
Time to appease my traveling consciousness.
On the divan I will translate for my companions
Verses of the *Tarjuman al-ashwaq* of Ibn Arabi
My heart takes on any form ...

If it were given …
For Kathy

If it were given I would speak the words
    in everyone's mind
Utter them with the rhythmic noise
that shakes open the shutters
ushering in the breeze
to stroke you with its fingertips
softer than wild rose petals
Or I would invoke the wind that rattles
and unhinges window panes
to waft you away
in full sail
if only for a moment
to be great among the great
small among the small
to be the poem that you are…

Cyprus

Marilena Zackheos is a Greek-Cypriot poet, scholar, and music maker. She grew up in Moscow, Beijing, Nicosia, Geneva, and New York City. She studied philosophy, creative writing, and English literature in the USA and the UK. She holds a PhD from George Washington University, Washington D.C. She is Director of the Cyprus Center for Intercultural Studies and Assistant Professor of Social Sciences at the University of Nicosia. She has published on postcolonial literary and cultural studies, psychoanalysis and trauma, gender and sexuality. Her music album *Oh My* was released in March 2017 under the band name Grendel Babies. Her first poetry collection *Carmine Lullabies* was published by A Bookworm Publication in 2016.

Red Light District, Geneva, 1996

When we were done he offered me a cigarette;
asked if I needed
	anything else
to love my body.

I thought about exposure,
		Prince Albert,
	Hafada,
Queen Victoria and Ampallang surfaced walls.

How people seek counsel in experience.
How true comfort lies in carnal taking.

Post navel infection,
		I found my way back
	to parlours: one in Cyprus,
another in New York.
I looked for penetration, the type he taught.

	But all the money spent got me
was a stud ejected
	from my eyebrow
and a bead
	that slipped from my tongue
		and passed through my gut
then I was back
where I had begun,
fixed on looking at the addition of scars,
			souvenirs
of the curse laid
	upon first-timers.

Orfeo and Heurodis

You pick me up, wash me off, untangle knots—pull my head
against your breast prosthetics.

They say a feeling of euphoria overwhelms Himalayan travellers
but perhaps it's due to high elevation.

You lavender, purify me, say "There are actually four states of matter:
solid, liquid, gas and plasma,"
I think, somehow this fact is of substance.

You dress me in my favorite black ensemble,
then I am no longer defenceless.

I practice *solitary ecstasy* – empty bottle in the right hand,
a timer in the other (sixteen, seventeen, eighteen);

until the end comes, I ask myself, If you could choose an appliance
permanently attached to your bed, what would that be?

I practice *sensual adrenaline* – lying naked, soaking the carpet
with slits in wrists (nineteen, twenty, twenty-one);

until the end comes, I ask myself, If you could ask Jesus one thing
before his crucifixion, what would that be?

I can't answer any of this so
you try: "a Nespresso machine" and "Dude, are you pissed?"

For Stomach-aches, Headaches, and the Like

In the dead city dip them in chocolate.
Freeze them in the Alps.
                                          Give praise to the cocktail party
    with the best dressed.
                      In the city that never sleeps
buy them Nat Sherman Mints.
    Let them rejoice with kiss-breath,
                            mosquito-bit skin.
In the half-city paint them white. Toss them over
    the green line.
                  Give praise to the child in the corner
    with a wooden-leg.
                  In the red city
carve them delicately. Place them within a series.
    Let them rejoice with eyes big as fried ostrich eggs.

For I was taught to doubt the words of strangers.
For I drew snake venom
            and spit it out in the stone cellar.
                                  For I was told
                  vitamins make you stronger.
For I wanted to be Mt. Olympus
        when all was said and done.
                        For I curse like I smoke cigarettes
but recollection is a mean bitch.
For when I concentrate on something long enough. For I have no regrets.
Bring forth a cliché.
    My God, I see you now.
                Translucent. Beautiful.
                    That night I played with your hair,
                      you called me *just a girl*,
then I turned snowy sheets carmine.
    I could do anything!
Remember?
    I trust you'll never tell,
    little girl,
    your optimism is what charmed me.

*All poems are included in the collection *Carmine Lullabies* (A Bookworm Publication, 2016).

Cyprus

Senem Gökel (1982) was born in Nicosia, Cyprus. Her first poems were published in Cyprus in 2005. Her poems, essays and translations have been published in various literary magazines in Cyprus, Turkey and Greece, such as *Varlık*, *Kitaplık*, *Isırgan*, *Cadences* and *Eneken*. Receiving the *Fikret Demirağ Poetry Award* in 2012, she has participated in a bilingual poetry book (Turkish-Greek) with her first poetry collection titled as *İkinci Jülide / Ζουλιντέ η Δεύτερη* (*Jülide the Second*). The book was published by the Cyprus Writers Union. Gökel has participated in various poetry anthologies and attended literary events including a poetry event titled as *Cypriot Poets: Transcending Conflict,* which she organized in collaboration with the National Poetry Library in London (May 2017). As of 2013, she is a student at SOAS, University of London, working towards her PhD in History with a focus on the history of medicine. Drawing in experiences from living in London, she has been noted describing herself as "the ghost of Bloomsbury."

On Sundays and the Stale Petals

I killed a glance
and wore it on Sundays
I resonated upon water
like the petal of a flower,
       staling in vase for days
I kept turning around. Then hushed.
I've left a leaky faucet behind;
we should have things to count at nights.

I got used to the sounds:
bees in the sunrise
garden bats in the sundown
sheets waving in the wind, like a whip
and the crackly creak of an empty swing
shaking the pole
     of my heart.

Translated by Zeki Ali

Wells on the Island

Let my delusions stay on the floor. I
want to gather my fears
and fill sacks with them.

Because you, wisely, explained
that you will take them.
That you leave them under the earth

and you shall return without them.
You said, I should wait for you with great patience.

Until, with a marble stone, you crash these visions
as if they were shells of almonds.

Then without looking back
I will pass the corridor

I will arrive at the kitchen for a glass of water
which I will drink in peace

without suspecting
that it comes from those wells

Those wells
Where the unclaimed bodies, along with their stories, were thrown.

Translated by Niki Marangou
Edited by Senem Gökel

Last Question
Dedicated to Setsuko Thurlow and the others.

Time does not age between the pages of a book
You poke it in a room
      to see
         if it's still alive

Even your dream has passed
Like the easily scattered petals of mountain tulips
You opened the door and closed it.

Get up
Surely there's someone calling your name

Japanese women have no fear
        of doors that rise as they get heavier

The bomb explodes and
      they fall in the sweet, feathery arms of the blue light

Someone is recalling the walking man
—his eyes in his palms

She splashes water to the Silence
—begging for *Water*.

Get up, for the sand

Release the embroidery hoop
        and turn it inside out.

A beanshoot is blooming in your head
A black beetle is hiding under the rock
A girl is writing on your walls in red

Cyprus

You lay your head on the pillow, like a pot
You caress her, like a pet

She is also asking
              for water.

Translated by the poet

Like a paramount of all miseries
I stood on the night of full moon eclipse
longer than any in last 120 years

Greece

Sotirios Pastakas was born in 1954 in Larissa, wherever he returned in 2012. He studied medicine in Rome and Psychiatry at Athens (Mental State Psychiatric Clinic). For thirty years he worked as a Psychiatrist in Athens. He published sixteen collections of poetry, a theatrical monologue, a book of essays and translations of Italian poets. In 2001 he co-founded the World Poetry Academy in the city of Verona, and in September of the same year received a scholarship from Hawthodern Castle, International Retreat for writers, near Edinburgh. He read poems in various International Poetic Festival (Sarajevo 2006 and 2011, San Francisco 2007, Rome 2010, Izmir 2012, Cairo 2013, Istanbul 2014, etc.) is a member of the Greek Writers Society from 1994 and has set up various print and electronic journals. Beyond editor but is a radio producer and teacher experiential writing. He has been translated into fifteen languages and the "Trilogy" book was released in the US in 2015, entitled "Food Line", translated by Jack Hirschman and Angelos SakisIn the spring of 2016 released a personal anthology of poems (1986-2016) in Italian "corpo a corpo" from Multimedia publications "Casa della Poesia", that win the NordSud International Prize for Poetry/Pescarabbruzzo foundation in 2016.

http://www.casadellapoesia.org/poeti/pastakas-sotirios/biografia

Nocturnal Readiness

Dreams of abandoned order keep me company
each night. The unfinished novel
of married life, the endless harping
on the same thing, passion and its painful
consequences: ready now, and in all conscience,
I must settle old scores,
get my own back, even though the digit clock
shows only 3.43: the present, I say, is
an illusion of a well-arranged past.
And yet, when I get up to sever
with my sword the sinister plot, I wear
my slippers back to front, and the last few
drops always fall outside the bowl.

Academy Street

As he walked down Academy Street, he didn't feel
the yellow acacia floret that came
and settled in his hair. He didn't realize
that people stepped aside for him to pass,
his way clear - green, too,
the next pedestrian light. He was unaware
of a host of erotic glances,
of smiles never returned, of faces
warmly beckoning with optimism,
Confidence, and kindness. Only when
he entered the lift did he blush with shame,
as he saw in the mirror the yellow floret
caught on his tie; and he smiled,
he, Tuesday's honored guest,
invested with the order of everydayness.

Evening Prayer

Dusk approaches to the rhythmic stride
of the teenager, who was left
alone under the basketball's open net.
The summer town's routine
gathers its voices a little beyond
and he glows with sweat
as he officiates with the chance equipment
provided by time: an orange ball,
a metal ring. Conceal
your glances, you passersby.

It's the body that loves itself
in an exclusive and passionate way.

Poetry from the Balkans

Yiorgos Chouliaras is a Greek poet & essayist, fictioneer & translator. In 2014, he was awarded an Academy of Athens prize for his Dictionary of Memories and his work in its entirety. His poetry in translation has been published in major periodicals and anthologies, including Harvard Review, The Iowa Review, Ploughshares, Poetry, World Literature Today, and Modern European Poets, and in Bulgaria, Croatia, France, Italy, Japan, and Turkey among other countries. Born in Thessaloniki, he studied and worked mostly in New York, before returning to Athens from Dublin. He has worked as a university lecturer, correspondent, press counselor, and advisor to cultural institutions.

Refugees

On the other side
of the photograph I write to remind myself
not where and when but who

I am not in the photograph

They left us nothing
to take with us
Only this photograph

If you turn it over you will see me

Is that you in the photograph, they ask me
I don't know what to tell you

Translated by David Mason & the author

Borges In Crete

We led him precisely to the point
where he imagined he had started.
The stones were intensely hot in the ruins
as the sun now penetrated everywhere
in a methodically uncovered past.
We looked without seeing.
Here must have been that labyrinth
he was telling himself lost in thoughts
uncorrupted by light.
Here it must have been entirely dark
just like now, he was saying, I can see it
while noisily the cicadas
sharpened the bull's horns.
He must have wandered to the exit
his hand tightly held in a ball
that its end was not visible
not now either if it existed.
Because we lost him from our eyes
in a moment as we were blinded
by the sun giving flight
in a mythical mirror to the real
idol of a nonexistent world.

Translated by David Mason & the author

Antigone

If not in the family
then where else
is the house of the dead?
If not without the state
then how else
is the denial of authority?
If not in death
then when else
is the wedding gift of life?

Translated by David Mason & the author

I must love this land
because I did not choose where to be born

Hungary

Katalin Ladik (Novi Sad, October 25, 1942 –) is a Hungarian poet, performance artist and actress. She was born in Novi Sad, Yugoslavia (now called Serbia) and in the last 20 years she has lived and worked alternately in Novi Sad, Serbia, in Budapest, Hungary and on the island of Hvar, Croatia.

She began her career in the early 1960s. Later she co-operated with art group *Bosch + Bosch*. She began experimental artistic practices and auto-referential performative exploration of 'gendered self' on the borders of intercultural territories of Serbia, Hungary. Parallel to her written poems she also creates sound poems and visual poems, performance art, happenings, mail art, experimental theatrical plays writes and performs experimental music and audio plays. Katalin Ladik explores language through visual and vocal expressions, as well as movement and gestures. Her work includes collages, photography, records, performances and happenings in both urban and natural environments.

Today her oeuvre includes written, sound and visual poetry; the visual arts, concept photography, performance art; happenings; experimental music; theatre, film and radio plays.

https://en.wikipedia.org./wiki/Katalin_Ladik

Hungary

Allow All the Trees to Grow!

Afterwards you can disappear. Already more have travelled
into the other reality.
This garden itself is the denial.
Already no human's face is visible.
Work-therapy-poetry. Everybody can cultivate it,
those especially who can match their heads to the horse's.
In this garden you too can disappear.
Since there will be less of us,
you can do a favor for those who follow:
with your art successfully exterminate the rats.
To be determined here, where the questioning
counts as ego tripping – your own enemy
are those who did history
fashioned after himself on an afternoon.
His madness pruned into you in a declared national park,
where even the worm counts as the opposition.
Reserved himself a seat, a ticket in the revolution.
This garden does not scream apples and peaches for you.

translated from the Hungarian by Emőke B' Rácz

The Hunt

The magnetic shaking of the blue needle: caution, Eden!
The horizon turns inward more
leading the self to the origin of the spring.
The hunter opens his sails
this delicious, fine mirror
tender, a hypnotic push is sent toward the untamed
the bird that sleeps in the burning mud.

Is there a cleaner beauty that feeds this flame?
You stepped into the garden through this door,
chasing you toward sin, more and closer.
You will feel the push on your wings
the hunter that sleeps in the burning mud.

translated from the Hungarian by Emőke B' Rácz

Hungary

Balkan Express

> *The returning worlds! as they*
> *turn with jagged edge around*
> *a no-matter-how falling minute*
> *that has to perish without me.*
>
> D. Tandori

Now I am farther from you than an ocean liner on the maize fields.
The telegraph posts rushing by are black masts.
I am too far to be torn like a victorious sail,
and I'll be still farther when I arrive.

Here there's thirst and a doleful voice from the deep.
The whole is but a dream – I whisper inspired.
An angel crashed here yesterday.

Now everyone writes a diary, they multiply history.
In the door a swan and a machine gun embrace.
The engine man has an ash-coloured face and hollow pits for eyes.

Farther and farther from you as I nearing you
a sparrow hits the window pane.
Big black stove-pipes start howling in me,
where are you? Here there's darkness and astonishment.
If this is history then I won't touch you,
don't wait for me at my arrival.

Translated from the Hungarian by István Tótfalusi

ISTVÁN TURCZI Ph.D. (1957)
Poet, writer, translator, university lecturer
Television performer of cultural and literary programs
The founder (in 1995) and editor-in-chief of PARNASSZUS poetry journal, director of PARNASSZUS BOOKS Publishing House.

Vice-president of Hungarian P.E.N. Club
Chairman of Poetry Section in Hungarian Writers' Association
Curate of National Cultural Fund

Prizes, honours:
International Poetry Prize in Warsaw, 2004.
Knights' Cross Order of the Republic, 2004.
National Prize of Literature, 2006. (József Attila Prize)

Main poetry volumes:
Auxiliary Muses in Black Lacquered Shoes, 1985.
Music for Unemployed Pianists, 1987.
Women & Poetry (erotic poems with photos) 1990.

As if motionless

A little statue appears in the stone forest of time: a female figure with braided hair and plaited robe, a bird on her shoulder. So ethereal, it could be a girl. Rarely touched by the sun; an enormous oak usurps its light. The girl, like snow seen through smoked glass. Not symbolic, not foreboding, just black. Perhaps the layers of the shadows make her appear darker, perhaps the observer just sees it this way. Today the girl is wordless, dolefully serious, and, like someone taking a long walk on the path alongside a lake, is not entirely the same as usual, somehow she is missing, *missing from there*; she longs for memories of old walks, for benches, clearings, in-between unsigned trees and blocks of stone quieter than she, who would like to cling to other winds and other scents, who would call to the coloured birds so unfamiliar to her, give them all kinds of nicknames and encouraging them, or rather encouraging herself, as shown by her half-baked movement, this shy uncertainty, oh, but why would she look back, she doesn't move, which she knows is not the same as being motionless, and in her acquiescence lies the hope that with each moment spent alone she might arrive, arrive at the Word, at the one able to unravel her braided hair, smooth the crinkles of her dress, and feed the black bird standing forgotten on her shoulder. They were fond of her once: she sat on fragmented rocks, amidst pebbles with a silvery glow, as she listened to the whispering of the dusk waters dipped in purple, she slept and danced, picked flowers and sang, prayed and loved, knew her body, the pilgrimage of blood, the rhythm of discovered movements, the repressed floating, the sounds lining up in words, the hot waves of her emanating breath, her shy smile, the lightness falling on her from the sky. She knew herself. That was when she lived as the grasses and flowers live; now she would very much have liked to see herself not being where she was, the black bird on her shoulder; she is not there, and neither is what happened next, what has already happened to her, and what has never happened and never will happen; in vain might that late afternoon sunshine break through the dense, merciless leaves of the old oak tree. She would like to have taken that long stroll on the path by the lakeside, one more time, one last time, to arrive at the opaque depths of the circularly whirling water, to arrive at her herself, at wherever, just to arrive there.

Let's Talk About Those Women Too

Let's talk about those women too
      who occupy an intermediate position between
        a lean to and a motel
they are the hosts of the underworld of my instincts
they have clear thoughts of fidelity bed anatomy
(I skip the details now)
they are trustworthy discreet duly banal
in exchange for my hired work they keep me like a king
they don't tire me with hot loving glances
they don't require much time don't nose after me on the phone
they have no compulsion to confess and no complexes
don't require spiritual hot-line and slippery romance

nothing   only the inarticulate speech of the body

so to warm up sometimes I tell them a healthy
horror story then they choke me tenderly
suck my blood slowly eat me up
and between two executions
with an off-duty hangman's pity in their eyes
        encouragingly stroke
        my disintegrating face

The Outsider

I looked in the mirror.
Since I have been on Earth, I've got a few millennia older.
Lava stopped flowing long ago; my features hardened to magma.
Along my mouth's line of flow the granite and gneiss are cracking.
Dinosaurs have become extinct from my eyes; even the continents
converge no longer. In my eye sockets lie lime and dolomite deposits.
This is the end. On my face, speckled with tiny islands, the stains
of oceans sink slowly: home to coral, to calcareous snails,
sea-shells, lobsters. On my temple, creases of mountains.
Since I have been on Earth, I've lost a modicum of energy,
my heat conductance isn't what it was, and of late I have
developed some kind of magnetic disorder. This is the end?
In my cells, radioactive decay has set in; the process,
it seems, cannot be undone. Put mechanically:
irreversible. This... is... the end. This may be the last
t e c t o n i c smile as I confront myself and Time.
Alone, my work not done, yet with ancient cheer I stand
before the mirror of creation, awaiting instructions, if any,
Lord.

Life is only a reflection of a real desire

Montenegro

Poetry from the Balkans

Tanja Bakić, born in 1981 in Montenegro, is the author of five highly-praised poetry collections, her debut being published when she was only 15, and the last one, *Sjeme i druge pjesme* (The Seed and Other Poems), in 2013. She is also a translator, holds an MA in English language and literature, writes as a music and literary critic. Her poems have been translated into fifteen foreign languages, presented at festivals abroad, published in international magazines and anthologies (produced in the UK, USA, Australia, Japan, India, France, Germany, Austria, Argentina, Greece, etc) and she has been awarded fellowships several times, one of these being the Central European Initiative Fellowship for the year 2016 (Vilenica festival Slovenia). The lecture she presented at the Tate Britain in London, entitled "William Blake in the Former Yugoslavia" is coming out published by Bloomsbury in 2019.

A completely ordinary man

Yesterday I bumped into you in the street
Under that same bridge
Where we used to hide together
From the rain and kissed
Twenty-five years ago.
You were carrying an umbrella
Which dropped out of your hand
When you saw my face appear
From nowhere before you,
Danijela.

You hadn't changed much.
You were still beautiful, as you had been back then
When you would read Prévert aloud to me
Or when, upon the creaky sofa
In my small rented flat,
You would sit next to me and catch my hand
Telling me how much you adore morning smells
Telling me how much you adore coffee.
But I would just let you talk
And ask you to close your eyes
So that I could descend the steps,
Leave the building
And purchase a sour cherry
Ice cream for you
Because you told me
You liked it best.

You haven't changed much, Danijela.
Except that the dreams you dreamt
About the big city lights
Took you straight
Towards them.
Tokyo, Rio, New York, Hong Kong,
Sydney, Colombo, New Delhi,
Casablanca, Moscow, London,
Cape Town, Toronto, Beijing.

Poetry from the Balkans

The years you decided not
to spend with me
In my shabby, rented flat
On one dead-end street
In a small quarter in Podgorica
You decided instead to stretch out
On the streets of the world's metropolises.
You met new people,
Had conversations with them
Different to the ones
You had with me.
You wore new high heels
Put on trendy jewellery
You looked into another sun
Every morning when you woke up.

But I was left making ends meet
In that same small flat
In a dead-end street,
Waking up early in the morning,
Going to work,
Getting back late in the evening
After having some wine
In a local pub.
Once a month
Paying my bills.
Once a month
Splashing out on
A train ticket
To the next town.

And so the snowfalls would come and go,
The winds, rains, storms and fogs,
Although my impression was
That for years everything stood in the same place
Except that you weren't here.
I had no idea where you might be,
Nor what you might be doing
But I knew you were a dreamer,
And that your dreams led you far away.

Montenegro

I still cannot forget visiting
Those packed cinema auditoriums
Together with you
I cannot forget
How back then you would tell me
How much you adored films starring Alain Delon
No, I cannot forget even that little gypsy girl
Who would approach us in the cinema
And tell us that were both good looking…
Twenty-five years ago.

I myself have never planted
A foot on another continent.
I have never seen
The big city lights.
I don't know important people.
I don't speak
Any foreign languages.

I am just a
Completely ordinary man,
With a modest
View of the world.
A man who can give you
Nothing but his
Small rented flat
In a dead-end street
In a poor quarter of Podgorica,
And the occasional night out,
An occasional nice word,
An occasional bowl
Of sour cherry ice cream.

You haven't changed much, Danijela.
Feel free to pick up
That umbrella which dropped out of
Your hand to the ground
When you saw my face appear out of nowhere.
Take it in your hands

Poetry from the Balkans

Open it back up
And just carry on walking
Wherever you were going.
And I will pretend that
I didn't bump into you just now.
I will pretend that I never knew you.
Oh, Danijela.
You haven't changed much.

Montenegro

You are gone

I sat on the edge of her bed
That hot July afternoon
I brought her a fruit yoghurt
The one she liked most.
The light from the window was falling
On the floor of the hospital room
In which she was lying.
And it was as if everything
Was made of marble
And it was as if
All over us
Some strange
Fog was descending.

You are leaving us
With invisible
But creaky footsteps.
Other people told me
You were leaving,
But I didn't believe them.
Other people told me.

I have collected
All the words you spoke
And am keeping them in a chest.
The sunflowers of your thoughts
Remain in my possession
Laid bare, then covered over.

Silent dust
Is slowly falling
on the marble around us.
And it is as if the air is missing
And it is as if
Many, many other things
Are missing.

I close my eyes and imagine
That now I am elsewhere, far away
That this here is not you
That this here is not me
That the hospital bed
On which you are lying
And this whole marble
Surrounding us –
Is just a tiny piece
Of a bizarre dream
From which at once
I desire to wake up
And open my eyes.

I quietly closed
The doors
Of the hospital room
And left on tiptoes.

The day after, they told me
You were gone.

I didn't believe them
That you had left

I still don't believe
You are gone.

A four-leaf clover

I stumbled across a four-leaf clover
Some twenty-odd years old
Placed inside page eighty-five
Of a primary school
Biology textbook.

The page was dog-eared
And yellow with dust, creased,
But as far as I can tell
The clover remained
The same as it had been back then
When I put it there
Twenty-odd years ago –
Pressed, flat, green.
I smelt it,
And instantly saw before me the little girl
Whom adults had told
That if she found
A four-leaf clover,
It would make any wish
Of hers come true.

And so the little girl
Found her
Four-leaf clover
In the grass
And she said her
Wish – big, yet small.

And so after all
These years,
Laid down
In the dust
In the closet of our
Dreams and thoughts
I somehow forgot
Whether the wish the girl had made

Had actually come true
In the meantime.
I cannot even remember
Exactly what her wish was.
All I know is that now,
When the girl stumbled across
Her clover
After so many years had passed by,
She rejoiced again
As she had done years before
When she saw it
For the first time in the grass.

All I know is that
She took her old clover
In her palm
Caressed it
Whispered to it a new
Wish – small, yet big –
And put it back
Into the same biology textbook
On the same page
Eighty-five.

Translated into English by Peter Stonelake and the author

Montenegro

Lena Ruth Stefanovic, poet, author and translator from Podgorica. Graduated from Kliment Ohridski University, Sofia.

MA thesis "In the search of paradise lost: Berlin novels by Vladimir Nabokov 1922-1937" defended in 1992.

Postgraduate studies of Chinese Language and Culture - BLCU, Beijing (1999/2000).
PhD thesis in Sociolinguistics defended on September 10th, 2014 at Pushkin State Institute, Moscow, Russia.

Works as Lecturer in Syntax at the University of Montenegro, Faculty of Philology, Podgorica.

Poetry - The Color of Change (Gligorije Dijak, 2013)

First Anthology of Montenegrin poetry written by women: Koret on the Asphalt (National Community of Croatian Montenegrins and Scanner Studio, Zagreb 2013)
Novelette "New Testament", Best European Fiction 2014 (Dalkey Archive Press, USA
Novel "The Daughter of the Childless One", Nova Knjiga, 2017.

The Devil
an autobiography

Do you not know me?

I am your adversary in this tale
That arrogant voice born of doubt
And fostered by fear.

I dwell in the constant storm
of your uncertainty
sprouting in the darkness
fed by your fury
and drinking up your pain
until you stumble and fall.

Still you dismiss me with a smile,
Denying my existence
As I bury you alive

Translated into English by Lena Ruth Stefanović and Stephen J. Mangan

Karadag

Ottomans called this land Karadag
the black land
where black mountains encircle
the black lakes
and woman with black eyes
save the black wine
for men with black moustache
when they come back home from the battle
in the Bright Dawn of May

Translated into English by the author

stalked by chronological narration

chased by master plots
haunted by the usual suspects
the characters of high brow prose
damsels in distress
and their cohorts
thorn apart by the cruel world
due sacrifices of the righteous people
of whom nothing less is expected
ever since the opening sentence
I run away from metamorphs,
barewolfs
and their maturation
from predictable fables of
strong lions' and cunning foxes'
irreversible transformations
bypassing allegories and metaphors
I hide
from conventional morals of the story
in the variable curses
of magical conversing
in unevenly rhymed verses

Translated into English by the author

Montenegro

Djordje Šćepović was born on 6 April 1983 in Titograd, Montenegro. He published the following poetry collections: Provinces of Salvation *Provincije spasa* (2004), Prayer for Judah/ *Molitva za Judu* (2004), A few words on fear/ *Par riječi o strahu* (2005), Apostle from the block A/ *Apostol iz bloka A* (2006), Three times say Metropolis, and feed the birds with letters /*Triput reci metropola i nahrani ptice slovima* (2009), As I drew the map of my travels (2016)/ *Dok crtah mapu svojih putovanja* and Before the Revelation/ *Prije objave* (2016). His poetry has been published in a number of poetry collections and anthologies, and translated into English, Hungarian and Slovenian. He is the co-founder and editor–in-chief of SCRIPT, Magazine for Literature and Culture. He lives in Podgorica.

As I drew the map of my travels

While in early morning
In a winter coat
And pain in my stomach
In a favorite café
I drink up my first coffee
And at the table full of
Ashtrays and daily papers
I draw the map in ash
Of my travels aback

A man will approach
And offer his skinny hand
And offer his shriveled open palm
Without a letter uttered
Without a sound written
Oh, no, I will not put a coin in that hand
Oh, no, I will not throw a coin to that palm
I could blemish his face
With a grimace of weakness
A grimace of vanity upset
May he go in peace
With fury on his lips

Reader

I am a reader in memory
From long ago, from the moment when shelves conquered the wall
My eyes move back from the letters
From an angry, wild hunt of ancient manuscripts

Dead is the one who reads and
The one who writes
Equally dead in forgotten paragraphs

I declare war to yet unwritten text
And though alone, I do not move back for a span
From a fiend who will pay
For all my dreams

Kerouac

I never read Kerouac
And why would I
And how could I
When they don`t have Kerouac
In the city library
I never read Kerouac
Instead of Kerouac driveling
For an afternoon pastime I would always
Choose fruitful woman`s thighs
Or bust at least
A collection of Kerouac for only one breast
I would swamp, if I had Kerouac
But I never bought Kerouac
And why would I
And how could I
When they don`t have Kerouac
In book salons
Kerouac is not in kiosk editions
Kerouac is in Alan`s shriek
In Alan`s hungry jaws

Chaser

In vain will they shoot the arrow
Parrot is always at least step ahead,
One wave of its wings will scatter the dreams
Of chasers and their gang

Its flash will not kill the hunger
Of bloodhounds, none of it this time,
They will return with empty hands
To their homes,

In vain their axes and spears,
They can`t toss far enough,
That Nymph will carry through the head
Rushing towards promised land,

In vain your traps, stuck in garden,
In vain your eyes, in anger red,
If bird even enters your cage,
Only then will it know how to sing

Translated into English by Vanja Šćepović

The fool who tries to understand Love
is the same with the one who has too many
clouds between two ears

Romania

Poetry from the Balkans

Mircea Dan Duta (b. May 27, 1967 in Bucharest)
Poet, film scientist and translator.
He writes his own poetic creation in Czech.
He published two poetry books:
Landscapes, Flights and Dictations (2014, Petr Štengl Editions, Prague)
Tin quotes, inferiority complexes and human rights or Married, no strings attached, selling dead born girlfriend (mention: worn-out) (2015, Petr Štengl Editions, Prague)
He is now preparing two new titles: *They don´t speak Polish in the realm of death* and *Regular client of the pub **At the Land of the Rising Sun**.*
His texts are also published in literary magazines and revues in the Czech Republic (Uni, Protimluv, Weles, H_aluze, Dobrá adresa, Polipět, Tvar etc.) and abroad:
- Dotyky, Literárny týždenik, Pars Artem, Revue Svetovej literatúry, Ilegalit (Slovakia)
- Suštnost (Bulgaria)
- Red-Hand Books / Balkan Poetry Today (Great Britain)
- Quest (Montenegro)
- Accente, Romania literara, Actualitatea literara, Urmuz (Romania)
- soon expected in Canada, France and Israel

The Cannibals

I fed on you,
for as long as there was something left to eat.
In fact, I somehow sensed
you would not be here for long.
Now they are eating me
And I have to be glad of it.
For as long as there is food for them,
It means I´m still here.
But you can no longer be aware of this.

Last Will

You will take her from me.
You will take it from me.
You will take everything from me.
In the end I won´t have anything left.
But you.
And I will still have to keep begging
to remain a part
of what will be yours.

While

Everybody wanted you.
I didn´t.
Everybody was looking forward to your coming.
I wasn´t.
Everybody was enthusiastic about it.
I wasn´t.
Everybody was glad to offer you the best
they had.
I wasn´t glad at all.
Everybody was congratulating us.
I didn´t find any reason for it.
And now it´s your turn.
Everybody wants it,
everybody is looking forward to it,
everybody is enthusiastic about it,
everybody is congratulating you,
everybody is glad to offer the best
they have.
And I don´t even know, whether you
want it,
are looking forward to it,
are enthusiastic about it,
consider it a reason for congratulation
and are glad to offer the best
you have.
And that´s because,
just like me,
you have never spoken.
You have never been capable
and I have always been afraid to say anything.
And what about him?
Neither you nor I know.
And even if we knew,
we still wouldn´t tell.

Poetry from the Balkans

Elena Liliana Popescu (1948, Turnu Măgurele, Teleorman, Romania) is Doctor in Mathematics and Professor at the University of Bucharest, Romania. She is poet, translator and editor, member of the Writers' Union of Romania and member of the Romanian PEN Centre. She has published forty books of poetry and translations from English, French and Spanish, both in Romania and abroad. Some of her poems have been published in Albania, Argentina, Australia, Bolivia, Brazil, Canada, Chile, Colombia, Cuba, El Salvador, Estonia, Germany, Hungary, India, Italy, Mexico, Mongolia, Nicaragua, Pakistan, Poland, Puerto Rico, Republic of Moldova, Romania, Serbia, Spain, Taiwan, Turkey, Uruguay, USA.

That instant

A few words, you told yourself,
just a few—and created
a story whose present
is yesterday by now, just as tomorrow
will be passed for another story
left behind,
lost forever...

One word, you told yourself,
just one— and you are on your way
the unknown,
that unexpected step, free
to think of who you are and are not,
of that instant in which you can become
and be you.

Hymn to Silence

He who still longs to put
his feelings into poetry,
Who is a guest at this royal banquet
inspiring his humble fantasy,

Who brings all he has as offering
to Him who is Life itself,
who forever returns to the sources
and learns anytime from the advice

Of anyone willing to teach him,
who dares look on in silence—
and find in random deeds
Him who, Alone, fully knows their pain

And keeps them alive through Love—
who tries to capture in poems
the living Essence hidden in secret potions,
extracting from Life's canvas

What the Painter wished to show
through shadows on the Face of immortality;
who dares to speak to humankind
with ephemeral verses

Dipping his quill in mute despair,
reviving hope and in words
laying all his love,
learning from all there is,

Who once had so much to say
with his contrived rhymes—
could he then write another poem
but for the one of endless Silence?

YOU

You, night of night,
who was before existence,
where life sprung
suddenly
because it had been there
always,
life that was to come
with time
through all lives
that are born and die
incessantly...

You, truth untold,
because mere speech
would hide you from
our unknowing eyes,
you live for us,
within us, unchanging,
forever...

You, sea of flames
that never burn, only heal
with their blazing light,
all powerful,
your purifying waves
transform the one who feels
in their murmur the pulse of life,
ebb and flow,
motion and stillness
whole and void, alike –
and yet
none of those,
indescribable form
that cannot be fathomed...

Poetry from the Balkans

My poem melts away
through the darkness surrounding you,
through the deepening fog
that forbids
even a glimpse
of your luminous face…

English version: Adrian G. Sahlean

Romania

Ofelia Prodan had her editorial debut in 2007 and has published several poetry books, among which *The elephant in my bed*, 2007 (the Debut Award of the Bucharest Writers' Association, 2008; Nomination for the *Mihai Eminescu* National Poetry Award - Opera Prima, 2008); *Ulysses and the game of chess*, 2011 (Romanian – English bilingual edition; Nomination for the *Marin Mincu* National Award, 2011; Nomination for the *Città di Sassari* International Literary Award, 2016); *The Guide*, 2012 (*Ion Minulescu* National Award, 2013); *No Exit*, 2015 (*George Coșbuc* National Award, 2015; *Mircea Ivănescu* National Award, 2016); *The snake within my heart*, 2016 (the *Poetry book of 2016* award at the *Avantgarde XXII* National Festival, 2017). She has been included alongside Nina Cassian, Nichita Stănescu, Ana Blandiana, Nora Iuga, Ion Mureșan, Mircea Cărtărescu, in *Voor de prijs van mijn mond* (Jan H. Mysjkin, Ed. Poëziecentrum, Belgia, 2013), an anthology that encompasses 12 Romanian poets of the last 60 years. An author's anthology has come out in Spain (*High*, El Genio Maligno, 2017). She has held public readings in Spain, Italy and Germany and has published in several foreign prestigious magazines, such as Nuovi Argomenti; Le Fram; Gierik & Nieuw Vlaams Tijdschrift; Asymptote and Tiszatáj. She is a laureate of the *Napoli Cultural Classic* International Award for Poetry and Prose 2013, 8th edition, winning First Prize in the category „*POESIA in lingua straniera*". She is a member of the Writers' Union of Romania and PEN Romania

the moccasin

a pathfinder has a moccasin. he is
the pathfinder with one moccasin. two pathfinders have
two moccasins. another pathfinder also has
two moccasins. if we've got 3 pathfinders,
will consequently have 4 moccasins. but if
we've got 4 pathfinders, I fly in a rage
and steal all of their moccasins.
there! I've stolen the lot and I'm utterly sad.
what am I to do with all them moccasins?
I go to the shaman, and the shaman gives me
some mushrooms. I gulp the whole lot on the spot out of hunger.
I start seeing all sorts of animals
and I experience creepy sensations.
the shaman tells me he is the pathfinder
with one moccasin and I am
the pathfinder with 5 moccasins and warns me not to forget
to return one moccasin to him
on my return from the world of our good ancestors.
after a while I do return hypnotized
and hypnotized I return the moccasin.
I leave feeling at peace with myself. on my way to the saloon,
I recover completely and realize
I am the pathfinder with 5 moccasins,
Yet I only have 4. I am beside myself.
I gulp down one litre of firewater,
then I go beat the daylights out of the shaman.
only, the shaman has ascended to the sky and
pulls faces at me from up there. he's mocking me.
I'm shaking my fist at him. he's victoriously shaking the moccasin back.

Robespierre's dream

Last night I dreamt
I was a louse
I dwelt beneath the wig of a French aristocrat
subsequently guillotined
I was, so to say,
a luxury louse
I'd accompany the French nobleman
to his perverse aristocrat lovers
subsequently guillotined
I used to study closely and with due admiration his seduction techniques
we'd be indulging in debauchery together
we'd be gorging ourselves on the most exquisite
fare together
and together we'd lose or we'd win
money gambling
my life was therefore carefree
true, from time to time,
my French aristocrat would scratch himself
with an ivory knitting needle
which bugged me no end
yet that wasn't the worst of it all
the worst of it all happened
once the Revolution began
and the poor fellow was caught
and subsequently guillotined in the public square
to the crowd's happy cheers
while I, overtaken with terror disgust desperation
and a variety of suchlike confused feelings,
took the plunge straight into the executioner's hair –
the executioner was a perfect yokel with plenty of lice of his own,
all of them dirt-poor and revolutionary
and thirsty for my blue blood
in their straightforward fury
they cornered me and without further ado
had me guillotined

Kafka's shoes

Kafka is tenderly watching his shoes
the shoes start slowly pacing to and fro in Kafka's sight

Kafka stoops to pick up his shoes
and goes out in the park to look at the world

as he sits on a bench Kafka is swinging
his bare feet and talking all sorts of
intimate things with his shoes

a fat policeman in a seedy uniform walks up
to Kafka threateningly swinging his truncheon and asks him
where he lives and whether he has documents for his shoes

Kafka produces the documents out of his pocket slightly offended
the policeman is checking them carefully then takes the shoes in custody
for further cross-examination

Romania

Anca-Mihaela Bruma strives to continuously challenge and change the world we live in by means of art, and it is by breaking away from old traditions that she invigorates the art world in pursuit of a new emotional intellect. It is central to her own belief that it is her duty to empower, motivate, inspire, educate and heal. The awakening of the latent gifts we all perhaps unknowingly possess is also central to her quest. In an astute and complex combination of art forms, Anca enhances the essence of poetry, bringing it to another level, creating a higher, more esthetic literary culture where creativity and logic abide in harmony. This, she succeeds in doing through the symphonic audio-visualizations which have become her distinctive trademark, where visual is visionary, mystical weds mathematical, and lyrical flirts with musical.

I Projected Myself in You

Thousands of times, millennia of evenings,
Myself I kept projecting in You,
So I can find the essence of the Truth…
To envision you a perception of Me.

I projected myself in You,
The seventh day of Heart to be seen,
A heart with no sleeps or doubts
In which the richest of the rich,
The poorest of the poor
And the greatest of the great
Travel through Love,
To find yourself in someone's mirror,
Neither in appearances nor labels…

Thousands of times, millennia of evenings,
Myself I kept projecting in You,
As I may remember the gnosis of the Heart
Pulsating the Universal Time,
Across the times, a marriage of Eternity,
To love myself in the silence of this cup
And find the mirror beyond my words…

The Autumn of Our Spring

My autumnal words fell on the sidewalk of Love!
You looked like Autumn… I behaved like Spring…
I found you when I had lost you
In this autumn… of our spring.

I re-arranged my rustic colors
so Love will gain a new anthem
with fluid steps and no numb regrets,
forgotten overdue epiphanies,
lost stolen rainbows
and red echoes with tangerine taste.

In this autumn of our spring
with its golden trail and acoustic wings
the season paints its words as a grand finale
while your leaves whisper secrets to the World
and a puff of wind lingers our photographic memories
as journals left and long forgotten on the path's end.

A stolen cry, a remembered loss of innocence,
as my desires hung on Sun's shoulder,
I see a repainted canvas of us
with cycled memories on the hills' canopy.

How sensual this autumn is!
Spiralling its space… tumbling its distance,
prolonged myself by flaming orange leaves.
During this autumn of our spring
my World turned into a September embrace,
October tinted your presence
With blossoming hues of green-orange undertones.

A dreamy dream… an autumnal fugue,
during lost Summer epopee,
and I breathed… with November pulse.
My soul's crimson is ambered and rubied
And I feel… autumned…

Poetry from the Balkans

I left my cinnamon spice to learn more about your beauty
the citrine embers of your eyes under the raindrops,
watched the cosmic dance on your skin, a whisper in time,
my temple of words still carry a forgotten white procession.

And love again… and again… dawns upon my future self
with rain scented winds, thrumming my life in your heart…

Words still scream the nuances of your disappearances
sailing across my punctuated flight…
Of so much yearning… I have sharpened more wings…

In this autumn of our spring, I will stumble no more
behind your voice… as Life cannot be sung half!…

A stolen cry… a remembered loss of innocence,
and I have learnt how to die… by living!…

Your Empirical Dominion

Through the glaciers of Time,
within extensive number of flashes and junctures,
in this steady and enduring intoxication
with its delirium surges and effluxes,
in the valleys where Knowledge does not need its knowing
and where the calculus towards the Infinitude
conceives the perfect curves and spherical realms,
unbounded, unconstrained with unbroken views,
where the Unseen is expanded by exponential dimensions
there… where illusions and desires have no more matter
no edge for yesterdays and tomorrows and past to be retold
as memory flames dance in verdant lush synchronicities,
I have unmistakably found you…
In the complexity of the simplicity!

Rudeness of word comes bitterer than absinth
More painful than kidney pain
More desperate than despair

Kosovo

He is on the verge of defending the doctoral thesis in the field of literature, in the University of "**Saints Cyril and Methodius University of Skopje (Republic of Macedonia).**

He's also active member of European Academy of Arts **(Academie Europeenne des Artes)**, League of Kosovo's writers and many other cultural associations.

He has published 12 books in different genres and a considering number of scientific articles on Karl Popper, Plato, Horace, Gjon Buzuku, Ismail Kadare, De Rada, Konica, Fan Noli, Migjeni and many other authors; about presence of the Bible in albanian and european literature, and some other articles from publicistic, art and culture, included in different books, newspapers and scientific magazines – with impact factor, too.

He is prizewinner of the Annual Award for Composition in Kosovo, 1992; Albanian Image in Education (from Forumi Imazh & Media), Tirana, Albania, 2014 and many other literary prizes in and outside Kosovo.

The poetry of Sarë Gjergji is included in many anthologies in Albanian language, English, Turkish, German, Romanian etc. His work has been a study object of many scholars. As a writer, he has been included in different literary lexicons. Participant in a lot of national and international conferences.

ARS POETICA

Variant I ~ Poetry

1
Do not abdicate from me
My soul is thirsty for you!

Do not take me for sinner
do not despise me for heresy
when inadvertently you ignore your requests!

Without your breath
I feel as an alive grave
Poetry.

2.
A mountain of metaphors is the book of poetry
trap of symbols
where at times there live
sperms of politicians and nations in agony
Pregnant cloudy earth ash and havoc
virgin whore and chants of saints
volcano storms, ghosts, wisdom of Solomon.
How many prophecy hides within
the Poetry-
fight for dignity!

Variant II ~ Poet

Come and see me pale on the face
Promised land of the arts on the night gown
White teeth on pieces of meat everywhere on the horizon
The world's tear in my eyes
In the pain that hides in every human cell
See the real face of the world, victorious on nothing

Between the poetry and a poet a universe separates, Poet
Here we have forgotten that in beginning was the Word
Disoriented in our paths
Border between ash and art we confuse
more evidence for the angelic face of evil.

Language of my father was depending
Poet…
Who does not mock with the art today?

Come again, please
Cause the word has fallen low here
In the dry land of our mind
Give the muse as a gift!

LANDSCAPE OF A LAND
Prayer to Mother Teresa

Come, on this earth
where criminals are made heroes
and the sanctity is damaged
where people have lost the taste
of water, soil and salt
where faithful love they do not want
neither the light.

Come here
where sacrifice is useless act
where Homer, Buzuku, Shakespeare, Baudelaire are profaned …
where alienation of mind alters the head
And the alienation of the soul converts the human being.

Come on this earth – the world of yours
that recognizes only generals
where it is played with your name
stuck in statue
where life is nourished with metaphors.

Come, I am pleasing you so, come once again
see how a man dies in the modern world
and how the elected of people cough
They have locked our Spirit in warehouses of parties
terra nulius – the value – ex nihilo…

O Come,
come and pray a lot
for priests and Muslim priests.

Poetry from the Balkans

Sali Bytyçi was born in Dejë, South East of Kosova, in 1962. He graduated at Prishtina University. M. A. in Literature. Ph. D. in Theory of Literature. Primary and secondary education has completed in Ratkoc and Rahovec while graduated in Albanian Literature Department of the Faculty of Philology at the University of Prishtina. In 2002 defended his master thesis titled "Funksioni simbolik i florës dhe i faunës në poezinë e sotme shqipe (1945-2000)" and in 2009 defended his doctoral topic "Vepra letrare e Azem Shkrelit" ("Azem Shkreli literary works") at the University of Pristina. In 1983 was sentenced by the communist regime for the offense -hostile propaganda and from 12 May 1998 until the end of October 2000 remained in prison: Prizren, Lipjan, Dubrava of Nis, as captives (prisoner of war).

From 1990 he worked as a teacher in primary schools in his district.Since 2004, in newspaper "Lajm" has held office of editor of the culture and linguistic editor, while since 2009 works at the Department of Literature at the Institute of Albanology in Pristina. With literary writings started during the study and has participated in scientific sessions that were organized within and abroad. Is a member of the Writers League of Kosovo and of the Association of Political Prisoners in Kosovo.

4912[1]

Yesterday I was a man
And today I may be a grave on the hill
I can be a lost one without a trace

Now I am just a number
A number that breathes
A number that rises in the morning and falls in the evening
A number that eats and sees
A number that moves on two legs

Now I am number 4912
That would be enough for me

Yesterday I was a man
Today I am a number
Tomorrow...

Prison in Niš (Serbia), April 2000

---

[1] In Niš Prison my personal number was 2194, which replaced my name, but for security reasons I've published this poem under the pseudonym, as well as several other poems under a different number, because sometime we received newspapers from Kosova, not as a regular newspapers but as a material wrapping food items, which when we put them together took the form of a newspaper. (Author's note)

When They Sentence the Poet

When they declare a poet
A terrorist
The Power goes mad

Middle Age heroes rise from the grave
And massacred children roam on the ground

When they declare a poet a terrorist
The smoke covers the sky
And the earth resembles more to Dante's Hell

When they declare a poet a terrorist
State kills itself
And people feed off with each other's heads

        Niš prison (Serbia), Summer 1999

Every time I think of You
to my wife, Drita

Every time I think of You
In front of my eyes I see ancient Penelope
And I am Ulysses roaming in the endless sea.

Every time I think of You
Before my eyes come a Girl waiting for years
                                                at home
And I am the soldier dying beyond
                Bridge of the Kaaba.

Poetry translated by: Fadil Bajraj

Bedri Zyberaj was born on 1963 in Drenoc, Rahovec. He finished his primary school in his hometown and high school in Rahovec. In 1988 he graduated in Albanian Literature and Language in the University of Prishtina. Until 1993 he was unemployed. From this year and until 1998 he was a teacher of Albanian Language and literature in his hometown. Parallel with teaching he would deal with issues of literature and journalism. In 1998, the publishing house,, Rilindja" in Prishtina publishes his first collection of poems,, Dromca vitesh"

After the last war 1997/99 (war of KLA) he has performed many important tasks in regards to his country and has been very active with literature. He participated in various roundtable and scientific conferences which were held within and outside Kosovo. In 2013, Albanological Institute has published his book with reviews and studies ,,Në gjurmë të arketipeve". He is a member of the Writers League of Kosovo (WLK). As of May 2014, he is director of the National Library of Kosovo ,,Pjeter Bogdani".

Besides the literary creation (poetry and prose) he also deals with literary criticism and publicist writings. Also, he has participated in different conferences Nationally and internationally, topics of interest to Albanian and regional culture.

He attended many poetry festivals in Kosovo and Internationally where he won many awards.

Despair

Our Lord
How strong we were when we wrote on stones
How anemic we are under neon lights

How faithful we were when we had swords
How much fratricidal we have become in the path of letters

How well we saw from the top of the mountains
How blind we are near chandeliers

Our Lord
How glorious we were in our smallness
How small we became with our glory

Prishtina,
9 December 2011

Anti-life

Buds of longing are budding from the end of the world of my soul
Comb of time combs flowers of the passed days
Stone of Sisyphus has its roots atop of the mountain
There's no one to push it downwards
Fruits of the tree of knowledge are rotten
Eva even though she wants them she can't eat them
From now onwards Adam will be bedridden in the Paradise
There's no God that will take care of him
The death of blessed solitude will get rid of him

Prishtina, 28 July 2015

Tonight

Tonight
Together with us is Homer
Sappho, Anacreont, Pushkin,
Baudelaire, De Rada, Serembe, Naim

Tonight when the vines lush
Poetry flows from the cauldron of brandy

In the light of the moon
Around the vine
Tonight
Lasgush is leading the dance of the stars
Khayyam is filling our glasses with Rubaiyat
Tonight
Wine is boiling in the cups
Rahovec is Eden

Translated by Fadil Bajraj

Bekim GRAICEVCI, was born in Prishtina, where he studied for drama. He actively deals with the production of documentaries, of many natural things; archaeological, prehistoric, different fate of the people living here, the shadows of unexpected changes and psychological relationships…

He writes Poetry writes from the childhood and has been published in the cultural archeology, prestigious here in Albany, in 1995 in the literature was rewarded with the first 3 voices in … the audition that was held that year, and a book was published, "to rescue love ",,- 'Ta shpetojme dashurine'

Overdose

Oh, how the years through me back
when we dreamt...
how much we dreamed,
Red cars Volkswagen...!?
America...Chaplin, James Deen, Jerry Lewis
(Those dreams, sweet and deep, how this lost river of underground takes them away, together with the white
of the pain, as this rain that drops, and as it becomes a moody river, silently suffocating us...)

Ever needed day is a step towards separation!...

These stains in the glass of the bus, how they turn me back to Monroe.
It is scratched with a knife M.M...!
a wretched child...
with legs lots of scratches and thorns within, when i raised in my feet, from the river, that I refreshed in summer times...
The bus stopped, in the dusty street...

Has any passenger got lost, while?
Imitating? James Dean, Jeri Louis or Morrison, that is freely circling in the Philippines?!!
This is how i hide behind God and my childhood dreams!
Me Proud

And a hidden Atheist and not alike you, that lie, only fear makes you human.

When i cover myself with the sheet i will pray, as a Buddhist monk
and i will curse behind the back, first them, that made me
as i spread my arms,
so i can reach a little your dream, my mysterious beauty!
I'm fed up, while seeing and eating my shadow...!?
i laugh, for the bad luck of the victim in absence, because it's you, but the devil saved you.
how well you know, but you don't accept it!!!

We the heroes of the bad luck state, tied:
In mechanisms pale of consumption
from pressure, anxiety, we silence, we are silent until death...!??
You need to eat your flesh, and speak not, you have to keep silent of hunger and to be silent, you need to piss,

right in the middle of the law right in the peak of constitution, so you can stop crying, so you can stop suffering.
Otherwise you will pay the sin buried alive as we are...

The sound of poop. when
we run in the streets.
so we can wreck our will, the waiting, the dream...
after it stops in the middle of intestine...
It hurts us, it burns in the middle of the stomach.
Ego, the fake.
Albanian!

Crisis cover us, sweating covers us.
in night without sleep.
we observe the dead space
and we lay as always, while drinking alcohol. speed, ecstasy...
This is how we meditate. get stronger we bite the steel. we suck the dick clitoris of a pussy...
thinking that we found the letter G!!
Right here we understand the deception, intrigue...
We always forget, forget tomorrow.
they burned our brain with restrictions
Oh, Oh, oh...
Like pathetic poets, wrecked like Greek Sufis!

We turn on the TV, recall the war we hear screaming,
Hysteria

I am def, blind, insane...
I promised you...
The returning in the dream!
I couldn't reach it!
They killed me in the middle of the road!?

It has no meaning, I tell you I'm sorry

And this asking for forgiveness its just a lie!
when I ran from the mirror, your face was red
And your eyes expanded

and this night likewise left us.
Then we smoked a cigarette and we kissed until we dehydrated

Kosovo

the nicotine covered our teeth and longs
the body started to bend

the ending, curiosity...!

how much i curse, i curse again
from the complex etno-psicho-Edip
They masturbate hiding in some corner
in a fiction with fairy tale dreams
of insane childhood
and listen songs for the homeland

we raised our two fingers, with naive faces in pictures...
it hurts me outside...!
The middle finger we point, to the enemy
We get fed up!

The dull moon, suspicion

and the time of dusk falls
we get red, deep red with politics.
we make myths, masked we fall in love...?!
We believe in God, magic, the fantastic miracle...

We rise, and we get by stairs with lots of garbage, a smell of a piss,
in the streets we meet and some food from those who help
we continue with steps, while measuring the doubts
and we stop from the spontaneous reflex, in the middle of the cross road
as always.
In front of the closed door, where in the station GETO
we wait like lost travelers of Dante like hell. Because Beatrice has got out of the book.

And we laugh and we laugh, from the complex-wrongly the hungry cynics
from the obsession moralized wrongly
we march showing our chest!
We don't believe in anything!
We give orders for killing,
and we go and pain, in some dark
..., Metamorphosis.

Bujar Tafa is a poet, essayist, literary critic and university professor. He was born on January 2, 1976. He has attended the primary and secondary school at Lipjan, and university, postgraduate and doctoral studies at Prishtina University (Kosova). So far he has published the following books: "Agim Spahiu's Poetry" (Prishtina, 2008), "Mirko Gashi's Literary Creation" (Prishtina, 2008), "Biographies and Ideograms" (Interpretation of Lum Lumi poetry book, Prishtina 2010), "Parapoetry" (Poems, Prishtina 2014), "Black Matter" (Poems, Prishtina 2016), "Literary contrasts" (Reviews, Prishtina 2016), "My Dardan King" (Poems, New York 2017).

The Traitor

In childhood I was a traitor,
a spy.
God forgave me.
At thirteen
I had my job.

Then hand in hand with the teacher
I drank cognac.
After that we visited churches,
then the citadel of skulls on the enemy land.

Then a neighbor woke up as a vampire.
Then a teacher
touched the girls' chest in school.

Then I grew up.

God Blessed The Poet

God blessed the poet,
gave him half freedom,
overwhelmed him with His love.
The poet is the Lord's choice.

He is above Christians, Muslims, Jewish.
The poet is a criminal,
President, filthy, capitalist.
Crazy, genius, cruiser, jihadist,
heaven, hell, mine, point,
the poetry is neither aesthetic nor ethical.

The time of bastards with square heads is over.
God blessed the poet,
the poet with half freedom.
And poetry is not the art of the beautiful word,
poetry is the poet's half-freedom.

It is the gift of the Lord for his protected servant.
Poetry awaits you, cuts you, burns you
with love, with fear.
It does not make sterile calculations.
It publishes pro bono.

Round And Round

It's not the earth,
no.
Spinning
around the sun
is my head.

Once a year
I turn my back on the sun,
entering the polar winter.
I feed the bears
with small, innocent birds.
It is not the earth, no.

That bizarre thing that's spinning
around the sun is my head.
Loaded with mountains, oceans,
deserts, intense traffic,
schools, hospitals,
heavy industry, hormones,
resorts, blood capillaries.

Once a year
meets my annual wish.
But I never see in a place
the shy sun
the same.

Photo credits to Branden B. Banko, Ljubljana, Slovenia, 2017

Fahredin Shehu is a poet, writer, essayist and Independent Scientific Researcher in the field of World Spiritual Heritage and Sacral Esthetics.

Born in Rahovec, South East of Kosova, in 1972, he graduated at Prishtina University in Oriental Studies. Passionate of Calligraphy, he actively works on discovering new mediums and techniques for this specific form of plastic art.

Some 17 books so far have been borne and his poetry is translated in English, German, French, Italian, Spanish, Polish, Serbian, Croatian, Bosnian, Macedonian, Roma, Swedish, Turkish, Arabic, Hebrew, Romanian, Chinese/ Mandarin, Bahasa, Bengali, Maltese, Frisian, Sicilian, and in several international literary magazines and anthologies such as THE WORLD POETS YEARBOOK 2009, Bei Jing, China, Poetas del Mundo, Santiaogo de Chile, Blue Max Magazine, Dublin, Ireland, Tribune de Geneve, Geneve, Switzerland, CHECK POINT POETRY, Le Reti di Dedalus, Italy, Anthology, Alquimia de la Terra, Ann Arbour Review, Michigan, USA, Coldnoon Literary Magazine, Jawhalal Nehru University, New Delhi, India, World Healing World Peace Anthology, New York, USA, Poetry in Anthology for the Rights of Hazara People, Oslo, Norway.

There

When you gaze up toward the forms of the white clouds
you find my face ablaze by the sun rays
mother or I am not...!?, wearing the brocade accoutrements
as in the bridal night,
with the hair anointed with lavender oil
with the face as a full Moon
in front of Venetian mirror
as in times when guns where shooting
while intermarry killing each other
as for who shall first pass the crossroad
between two cemeteries
one of the Plague and the other of children dead
                                        by Measles

today when I bow down my sight and see my stomach
                            while earth is dragging by
somehow as I want to sing the song of the Midday
when the Sun vanishes your shadow
and the Bachelors faint
while looking bare feet escape of the Fairy with the inflamed
                                           curly crest
the fragrance of Myrrh and Violet spreading all around
as in times when the Moon was adored as God
while Pagans prayed for the rain to fall
with bells and kelp,
elder leafs and bowing boughs
of the weeping willow folded
tomorrow we shall look straight in the eyes
seeing the lie of each other,
how it leaks as mercury in aged veins
with antimony poisoned while juvenile
and our faces will not blush out of shame
because we folded the darkness in rule
we bind it in a sack woven
        in the Loom of the Sun
there where you drink the vine that never makes your drunk
where Love is done as breathtaking
and isn't nominated as we do
there where the Word is done not uttered instead...

We knew not the separation

Statured amidst dews of petty things returned refreshed with
lungs full of Myrtle and Pine fragrance,
seeking serenity in a grotesques trammeling of worn– out Spirits
I roam, jostling fears and hopes and forgetting brand linen I ought
to wear– the only thing to be buried with…and the linen written all
over with Saffron and Rosewater all of my poems I was unable
to write on Friendship, for the poet's sensitive Soul who once lived
in the Constellation of Peace- the same I want to rebuild here,
and the bright stars felt upon wombs of our mother's shall bear witness.
One day when from the bleach-white or rather Neon– light
skeleton of mine, the shine shall emit the rays from the sky– wide dome.
Again I returned from the mossy ruins I was seeking the Beauteousness
of your being and you remember the wine we drunk even before
we knew not the separation. And there was none. As the souls of ours
merged long time ago and for eternity and a day more.

From NEON CHILD
Inner Child Press, 2018

5.

Bloody ignoramus
They thought I am a stone
They thought I am a plant
They thought I am an animal
They thought I am Jinni
They thought I am an Angel
They thought I am an Angeloid
They thought I am a Salamander
They thought I am Daemon
They thought I am possessed
They though I am a lunatic poet
They thought I am a soul gambler
They thought I am holy indifferent
They though I am a New Age Templar
They thought I am a Muslim
They thought I am a Christian
They thought I am a Hebrew
They thought I am a Buddhist
They thought I am an Ascetic
They thought I am an Urban Eremite
They thought I am an Urban Pilgrim
They thought I am an Astral Projection
They thought I am a Hologram
They thought I am Fata Morgana of icy desert
They though I am Morgan le Fay
They thought I am Lilith
They thought I am Ahura Mazda

But I am what "I am"
A Neon Child

While your god punished
mine was busy making Love

Macedonia

Photo by Alexandar Ivanovski 2013

Katica Kulavkova (Ćulavkova) was born in Veles, Macedonia, in 1951. She is a member of the Macedonian Academy of Sciences and Art (since 2003), a member of the European Academy of Sciences and Arts (Salzburg, since 2014) and Vice President of PEN International (since 2008). She lives in Skopje (R. of Macedonia). She was working as a professor of Theory of Literature, Literary Hermeneutics and Creative Writing at the University of Skopje.

She studied literature at the University of Cyril and Methodius in Skopje, at the University of Zagreb and at the Sorbonne in Paris. Her first book of poems appeared in 1975. Since then she has published more than thirty books of poetry (in Macedonian and in many translations) as well as two collections of short stories, one play, and approximately forty other books as both author and editor. She has received numerous Macedonian literary awards.

Confession

"I know not what confession is, a true one.

Something drives me
to invent
to exaggerate
to withhold
to add
to rearrange
to change

yet, the hoof of
dying
paws at me
and I am not hiding that
my drives
are flowing in all directions
even now,
to the left, to the right,
out of their berth
rising like well-kneaded dough
like shaken champagne

Every night I wait to hear
God's voice between the lines
not to forget the dream
before I've remembered it

(my memory has overflowed
it shot up, it boiled over
a volcano cannot measure up
a fiery force of nature flows)

- *a kingdom for a good poem* - [2]

---

[2] **In reference to** William Shakespeare's "A horse, a horse! My kingdom for a horse!" in *Richard III* (Act-V, Scene-IV).

I forfeit consolation even
so long as verse by verse, the verses
are prompted to me
by That One, there Beyond
The Cherry Orchard". ³

Translated by Jasmina Ilievska-Marjanovic

---

³ A subversive interpretation of the role of the prompter as divine voice in any theatre play (thereby in poetry and in the arts in general), but here Anton Chekhov's *The Cherry Orchard* is pointed out.

Confessions of a Child

"I do not know why the strange feeling
that each day is my Judgment Day

so my skin crawls from fright
and shivers overtake me
and I get myself entangled, as a long
extremely long and old thread
full of knots, without the patience
to untie them!

Then I come to my senses, unaware
returning with a time machine
to the virtual reality
and I continue playing
and imagining

for how else am I to survive, Mom,
I don't know!"

Translated by Bela Gligorova

Each Morning

The day and the night
when setting up boundary marks, in delirium
return each other their bodies:

proof is the sperm splashed
in the semi-sky, semi-earth[4]
(wake up, get excited
tomorrow around 4 am
go outside in the open
and have a look!)

The day dawns alone
like every experienced lover
– as if nothing (though everything) has happened
at the same time
within them echoes the sultry sexual speech
of his host's
and of her hostess's
hospitality.

In the morning the mountains should be licked
generously, tickling, from within
Along the saddles, the passes, the peaks.

God-given tongues we have
for the heavens and the earth
under, over, in front and after
the inhaling should be deep, so as
to alleviate the gush of the daytime silence beforehand
until our next meeting with the nocturnal grammar.

The day and the night are doing it
all day and night, as decreed by the house code
of conduct – the Time.

Translated by Jasmina Ilievska-Marjanovic

---

[4] "Semi-sky, semi-earth" (half-sky, half-earth; part-sky, part-earth; the space between, bordering earth and sky), but in Macedonian the word „пол" /pol/ besides meaning "half, part, semi-" as a prefix, by itself it also means "pole"(opposite poles, +,-, South/North Pole) and "sex" (being male or female), so the verse in original („на пол-небо, на пол-земја") could also carry these layers of meaning.

Macedonia

Nikola Madzirov (poet, essayist, translator) was born in 1973 in Strumica, Republic of Macedonia, in the family of war refugees from the Balkan Wars. His book *Relocated Stone* (2007) was given the Eastern European *Hubert Burda* poetry award and the most prestigious Macedonian poetry prize *Miladinov Brothers* at *Struga Poetry Evenings*. Other awards include *Xu Zhimo Silver Leaf* award for European poetry at King's College in Cambridge, *Studentski Zbor* award for best debut in Macedonia and *Aco Karamanov* award for the book *Somewhere Nowhere*. The contemporary jazz composer Oliver Lake has composed music based on Madzirov's poems. Nikola Madzirov was granted several international fellowships: *International Writing Program (IWP)* at University of Iowa in USA; *DAAD* in Berlin, *Marguerite Yourcenar* in France or *Passa Porta* in Brussels. His poetry has been translated into more than thirty languages. Mark Strand wrote: *Madzirov's poetry is like discovering a new planet in the solar system of the imagination.* His book in English, *Remnants of Another Age*, was published in USA by *BOA Editions*.

After Us

One day someone will fold our blankets
and send them to the cleaners
to scrub the last grain of salt from them,
will open our letters and sort them out by date
instead of by how often they've been read.

One day someone will rearrange the room's furniture
like chessmen at the start of a new game,
will open the old shoebox
where we hoard pyjama-buttons,
not-quite-dead batteries and hunger.

One day the ache will return to our backs
from the weight of hotel room keys
and the receptionist's suspicion
as he hands over the TV remote control.

Others' pity will set out after us
like the moon after some wandering child.

Home

I lived at the edge of the town
like a streetlamp whose light bulb
no one ever replaces.
Cobwebs held the walls together,
and sweat our clasped hands.
I hid my teddy bear
in holes in crudely built stone walls
saving him from dreams.

Day and night I made the threshold come alive
returning like a bee that
always returns to the previous flower.
It was a time of peace when I left home:

the bitten apple was not bruised,
on the letter a stamp with an old abandoned house.

From birth I've migrated to quiet places
and voids have clung beneath me
like snow that doesn't know if it belongs
to the earth or to the air.

Separated

I separated myself from each truth about the beginnings
of rivers, trees, and cities.
I have a name that will be a street of goodbyes
and a heart that appears on X-ray films.
I separated myself even from you, mother of all skies
and carefree houses.
Now my blood is a refugee that belongs
to several souls and open wounds.
My god lives in the phosphorous of a match,
in the ashes holding the shape of the firewood.
I don't need a map of the world when I fall asleep.
Now the shadow of a stalk of wheat covers my hope,
and my word is as valuable
as an old family watch that doesn't keep time.
I separated from myself, to arrive at your skin
smelling of honey and wind, at your name
signifying restlessness that calms me down,
opening the doors to the cities in which I sleep,
but don't live.
I separated myself from the air, the water, the fire.
The earth I was made from
is built into my home.

Poems from
REMNANTS OF ANOTHER AGE
(BOA Editions, 2011)
Translated in English by
Peggy and Graham W. Reid

Macedonia

Lindita Ahmeti was born in Prizren in 1973 and lives in Skopje. Her first poetry collection, *Mjedra dhe bluz* (Raspberries and the Blues), Skopje 1993, was well received. Ahmeti, among the best-known female poets of the Albanians in Macedonia, is the author of seven volumes of verse: *Ishulli Adular* (Adular Island),1996; *Brezi i Zonjës* (Rainbow), 2000; *Vetë përballë Erosit* (Alone in front of Eros), 2004; *Nga Mështeknaja e babait* (From the birchwood of my father), 2015; *Dhoma pa derën dalëse* (A room without exit door), 2015

Memoirs

Before the small houses in Gazi Baba
The old men gather in the alley,
How white
In the muddy square.
There they disperse their memoirs
O'er the asphalt,
Never red, never black,
And marching, surging,
The Turks,
The first Serb,
The first Bulgarian,
The second Serb,
The second Bulgarian,
Greeks, Greeks, Greeks,
Byzantium, Asia,
And Europe locked
In Scanderbeg's grave,
All the while, the old men squat
Before the small houses in Gazi Baba.
Translated from the Albanian by Robert Elsie.

Letter to my Brother

Nothing new going on here, brother,
Everything is just as it was,
The new trees are infected by a fungus,
As always
The flaking whitewash falling off the wall,
As you know,
Joseph's mother has come back.
The same things are happening
In the bramble bushes.
I alone have changed,
I alone strain to hear your voice,
For example,
When you'll return.

Translated from the Albanian by Robert Elsie

Who Will Bring Word to Me

At the Balcans, the door open,
I am waiting,
A year, a century,
God, a grey year,
A terrible year,
A deaf year,
I am waiting,
Centuries spent waiting,
The year makes no move,
Wedged between the hands of the clock,
An ominous hour,
And I keep watch,
Nowhere the racing pigeons,
The postmen felled by smallpox,
I look through the gaping door,
A coat of dust on the grass,
Silt in the trees,
Who will bring word to me?

Translated from the Albanian by Robert Elsie.

Macedonia

Lulzim Haziri (Gostivar, 1962)
Poet and writer.

Poetic bibliography:
Kënga lind në vetmi (**The song was born in solitude**), 1989, Rilindija, Pristina
Kur dyert happen me zile (**When the doors open with rings**), 1995, Vatra, Skopje
Dalja nga safari (**Exit from safari**), 2005, Brezi 9, Tetovo
Vetmi e varur si numër në portë (), 2016, LogosA, Skopje
Кога љубовта се троши како креда (**When the love is wasted as a chalk**), 2017, GOTEN, Skopje, translated poetry into Macedonian language.
Literature:
Rokenrolli shqiptar! (**Albanian Rock and Roll!**), 2000, Shkupi, Skopje
Bardhë e zi (**Black and White**), 2010, Nositi – Sh, Gostivar

Morning song

Fed up with the nocturne written at mid-day
I woke up with the first sunshine
Together with the cockcrow of self praise
I opened my eyes and looked through the window
The fluorescent light spread out its arms
All the way to infinity
The traffic lights winked
The city buses hurried heedlessly
The passers-by carried their severed heads
Their hands searching pockets full of illusions
Newspapers sticking out of their rims
As the most efficient cure for the lack of communication
In this age of eclipses
When the nocturnes are written at mid-day

The sun hangs at the zenith
Marking the end of the market day
When with dark glasses on my nose
I set out search of the singing cocks.

Translated by Zoran Anceski

The Birth of the Song

The lonely people are like zeros
You add them
You subtract them
Never One
Never Two
Or Three
The zero follows them
But they are not zeros
The lonely people don't eat Time
Dry
They write letters with tearful eyes
And never mail them
Loneliness does not stamp them
It makes you hang yourself on a line of words
And like a scratched record chants repeatedly
The song is born in loneliness
The song is born in loneliness
The song is born in loneliness

Translated by Zoran Anceski

Busts

The sculptors were not bothered by their real appearances
but the bronze men were handsome anyway
the leaves above them were made anxious
as were the freezing lovers beneath them
by their bronze silence
But the stage curtain lifts up
and those handsome men are removed on tractors
their eyes of metal looking broken
while watching the streets and the squares
saddened by the betrayal, the lies, plots and hatred
The neglected busts are most attractive
when a pigeon or crow drops some shit
on their regular nose and when
the garbage collectors pay no attention to it
Even myself feel offended when wiping it off
An old man comes along the alley and waves his stick
at the nose of a bust, saying: "This thief stole two of my cows!"

Translated by Zoran Anceski

Macedonia

Daim Miftari is born in 1979 in Gostivar, Macedonia. He holds a masters degree in Albanian language and literature at Skopje University. Currently he lives in the multilingual city of Skopje, where he has worked as journalist, translator, and teacher. A number of published books in both Albanian and Macedonian, as well as poetries translated and published in antologies, newspapers and literary magazines in Macedonia and abroad, have earned him acclamation by the literary critics. In April 2017 Miftari was granted literary residence POETEKA in Tirana, Albania.

Morning

The city woke up
and went out for a walk.

Last night it had slept
earlier than usual.

At some later hour
I sat sipping coffee.

We meet rarely nowadays.

We nod to each other in
passing
as if we were
some slight acquaintances.

There May Come a Day

there may come a day when I cry out
kind of annoyed
to hell with all my poetries
written and unwritten
I'm so tired of them
putting each word on its proper place
in each sentence
much like a kid lost in his gaming world
and I sure was happy just as one
each time I believed that I had made it
and then just like a kid respawned
thinking sure
I could be doing something else
easier perhaps or more useful
than wasting my time like this
but simply realizing
I am not really skilled to do anything else
If It Wasn't Me

if it wasn't me

someone else would be living
in the apartment where I live today
in the same city
on the same street
at the same address
and those days would be quite the same
with all the seasons inside
all the happenings
joys and sadness's
happiness's accidents foolishnesses
like loaded trucks

if it wasn't me
someone else would be standing
at the same balcony where I stand
late at nights at times
watching the street fall asleep
like a tired traveler
under neon lights
and shadows of trees

suddenly his thoughts would fly
across the mountains
to a childhood home
that he too might have abandoned
and to some dreams
teared apart like old clothes
by some stubborn tree branch by the street
and to his word
his given word
that he would love her and cherish her
forever
and later on he'd ask
where did she disappear
her joyous stare
her thin laughter
and sometimes like a bird
on an April-green branch
sadness would rest upon her face

Macedonia

if it wasn't me
someone else similar to me
would suffer to the bone
frauds injustices
revenges greed
losses unfaithfulness's
and upon feeling tired
from the urban noise
to put his head to rest sometimes
he would also hide
far, far away

if it wasn't me
someone else like me
would have friends
to go out with
and the world would seem nice at times
and sometimes he'd spit on it
and he'd hate his bad fortunes
for not being living somewhere else
where he'd be better off
with his family

because he would also be married with kids
and would go out with them at the weekends
and carry about them
and worry about them
and their future
and play with them
at the evenings and read them tales
and often trapped
by some curious question
try to find answers

when his kids would grow up he'd tell them about life
and his past
his loves
his dreams
his regrets
and against his will a tear would drop
like water gathered from tree leafs by the wind
after a crazy rainstorm

and still he'd say
he's happy anyways
with everything he's accomplished in life

he'd have a library full of books
to read
any time he'd get a chance

or perhaps he'd have another trade
it's mustn't be poetry

Serbia

Gojko Božović (1972), poet, essayist, literary critic, editor and publisher.
Books of poetry:* Underground Cinema *(1991),* Soul of the Beast *(1993),* Poems of Things *(1996),* Archipelago *(2002),* Elements *(2006),* Nearby deities *(2012),* Map *(2017).

Book of essays: *Poetry in Time: On the Serbian Poetry of the Second Half of the 20th Century* (2000), *Place We Love: On the Contemporary Serbian Poetry* (2009).

Anthologies: *An Anthology of Recent Serbian Poetry: The Nineties, The 20th Century* (2005), *Place We Love. An Anthology of Contemporary Serbian Poetry 1945-2006.* (2006, 2011; in English), *The World around Us. An Anthology of Contemporary Serbian Stories* (2009).

His poems and essays are translated to English, French, Italian, German, Russian, Czech, Portuguese, Hungarian, Dutch, Danish, Slovenian, Norwegian, Polish, Bulgarian, Romanian, Slovak, Bulgarian, Greek and Macedonian. He received the awards „Dušan Matić", „Brana Cvetković", Djura Jakšić", Branko Ćopić" and Europa Giovani International Poetry Prize" (Italy) for poetry. He received Borislav Pekić Fund Award" for essays. He is founder and Editor-in-Chief *Arhipelag Publishing* (Belgrade, 2007) and *Belgrade Festival of European Literature*. He lives and works in Belgrade (Serbia).

Besieged City
Virgil, Eclogue IV

"And once again great Achilles to Troy shall be sent,"
And once again Troy shall be discovered
In every place where
Great Achilles turned
Into the child of his anger,
Into the parent of his madness.
And once again arms shall be forged,
The world shall shine in the shield's morning,
Mute iron shall begin to speak in the squares,
And once again shall cities be besieged,
In the besieged cities one shall exchange
Days for nights, and days for years,
Kingdoms for submissiveness,
And once again walls shall be torn down,
So that we can, finally, return home,
Among the unknown household members,
So that the besieged city be built once again.

Translated: Dragan Purešić

Last Photograph with Father

I have not kept
The last photograph with my father.
We were sitting in my father's car,
And I was silent,
He was talking and breathing heavily,
Struggling for air.
What is left of the photograph
Is just a strip of light,
Although it is more important to me
Than the preserved photographs.
But I remember
That I was looking right ahead,
With my eyes wide open,
As if I could see
What was coming.
What had already come
And placed itself between us,
In my father's light-yellow car.

Translated: Dragan Purešić

Above water

I felt we were sinking.
Water penetrated ship's foundations,
Water, oily, black water,
Heavy as the earth itself,
While we were leaving the deck
In unresolved dispute
Descending into the underworld,
Through water and mud,
Imagining the limits of the lower deck
As the limits of a terminated world.
And nobody would look up
To keep head over water
And examine the contours of the island,
Promise of a distant land.
I felt we were sinking
Something more powerful than water lured us into water.
Something as old as water.

Translated: Radmila Nastić

Poetry from the Balkans

Dušan Gojkov is a poet, short story writer, novelist, essayist, journalist, radio drama director, the founder and the editor-in-chief of the Balkan Literary Herald.

He published 15 books of prose, dramatized and directed for radio around 250 prose and poetry works, and has reported for the Yugoslav press from 37 countries.

Poetry of Dušan Gojkov was published earlier at: **Copenhagen Review**, Kopenhagen, Danmark; **Knjigomat**, Zagreb, Croatia; **Jellyfish Whispers**, Daytona Beach, Florida, USA; **Primorska Srečanja**, Nova Gorica, Slovenija; **Zetna**, Senta, Serbia; **The Missing Slate**, Islamabad, Pakistan; **Penny Ante Feud**, Charleston, South Carolina, USA; **Lirikon,** Velenje, Slovenija; **The Criterion**, Mumbai, India; **Libartes,** Beograd, Serbia; **Both Sides Now,** Tyler, Texas, USA; **Radio Gornji grad**, Zagreb, Croatia; **Балкански књижевни гласник – Balkanski književni glasnik,** Beograd, Serbia; **100 Иљади поети за промена,** Strumica, Macedonia; **Политика**, Beograd, Serbia; **Свеске**, Pančevo, Serbia; **Zarez**, Zagreb, Croatia; **Путеви**, Banja Luka, Bosnia-Herzegovina; **World Poetry Yearbook**, Chongching, China; **Pesmi, izbor iz srbske poezije,** Koper, Slovenija.

poem № 4

she
sadly packing winter clothes in the closet
trying to remember
where has she lost the past year
which was the first and last for many things
he
leaning against the bed
writes meaningless pathetic verses which do not even rhyme
but actually trying to remember
how and where the heck did he lose the past year
he comes closer to the window it's spring time
the street is dark and there is no more light, golden and grainy, from the wooden pole
that light that smells of fresh warm bread
and of winter
do you remember that some time ago we planned to travel to Paris
and we still haven't gone
together
you say your tea is getting cold
it's good to write poetry
you always have at hand a little piece of paper on which you can put the seeds from the cherry dumplings

the vernal

I know that the poplar beneath your window
is shooting
young leaves
and that the magnolias and tulips
across the road
are in blossom
yet I give your street
a wide berth
as, gods knows why,
I remember the beautiful vow
we made long ago:
"my body will wait for yours
under a rock somewhere"—

by what accident
through which torn pockets
did we ever lose
those mornings
the grey ones
the warm ones
mornings of every kind
those evenings
spent to a glass of wine
quiet music
and glances exchanged
through sunlit eyes
those nights
in which I was
calm, quiet,
curled up next to you

on the other hand
the rumors are true
I still manage
to bring a smile to a woman's face
every now and then
and some of them even venture
to my distant suburb

Serbia

for no other reason
but to bring me chocolate
fruit cake
a bottle of wine
a new book
to have a cup of tea
or a different drink

" life goes on"
say the wise
but I suspect that
those pictures
which spin around me all night
and all day
that hole in my guts
that void in my heart
will not be mended by time
or modern medicine

I know
we have wasted much
deliberately or accidentally
much that we could have done
for each other instead
I know, I know

under a
vernal
drizzle
I slide down Lorca street
(it is quite clear that new shoes are
long overdue)
I arrive home
feed the turtle
sit in the armchair
taking strict care not to
look at the corner of the room
where your painting gear used to stand
your easel
canvasses
paints
brushes

and things

on the table next to me are
a bottle
a glass
coffee untouched since this morning
and a vase
with those weird little yellow flowers
I can never remember the name of
which (OK, I'm ashamed)
I stole for myself last night
from the little park
across the road

I light my cigarette
gaze at nothing in particular
and let the yellow petals
quietly shed on my shoulder

other people's memories

I remember
portobello road
where I first touched you
to draw your attention
to a beautiful façade
the passers-by
were running from the rain
the fruit-sellers
closing their stalls
I remember
the church portal
where we listened to
the warmth of silence
I remember
watching you sleep
with your lips puckered
and listening
to your deep breathing
I remember the sheet
over your hips
in a tender
outline
interesting
I can't remember
what your eyebrows were like
I remember
the row of trees
which cut through the vineyard
the persistent wind
and the way we walked slowly
with your hand
in the pocket of my coat
Listen
this may sound corny
but before I met you
there was really something missing
I remember
your letters
blassblaufrauenschrift
which you left on the pillow every morning

while I was still asleep
I remember
how you waited patiently
for me to finish
looking at three paintings by Monet
and remember
watching you dance
to music
all alone
and our long walks
in the streets around the covent garden
I remember us
in a train
tangled together, sleeping
as we travelled
or our little room
for rich tourists
above the café de la paix
too expensive but that's what you wanted
the square
was teeming with people
I remember
the record that played
on and on
over and over again
(tom waits, closing time, I think)
I remember
holding your hand
when you were afraid
I remember
the restaurant with the name I've forgotten
but which I could
still find
with my eyes closed
and our silence
stretching for hours
to a bottle of wine
hell, that was an ugly silence
and this is the book
I bought that Saturday
when I waited for you to finish at the hairdresser's
the streets were moist

Serbia

with last night's rain
or the street washers' efforts
it was early morning
still a bit nippy
and we went
to have coffee together
but we didn't have coffee
because we had to shout at each other a little first
so things felt awkward afterwards
I remember you
watering the flowers
singing to them quietly
so they would grow better
and how, cheeks flushed, after work,
you downed a tumbler of cognac
to which I objected
hey
have some respect
that's good stuff
I remember
the spring in Greece
when you sobered me up
with olive oil and vinegar
disgusting
you followed the advice
of the women in our neighbourhood
that's how they tortured
their husbands
then came the summer
and the two of us, sunburnt,
lay prostrate in our room
with a big wet towel
across our backs
and we whispered: listen
the heat is so strong that it buzzes
at night
we sat on the terrace
nuzzling the cold chenin blanc
that's when we discovered it
I look at your profile
as you take your shoe off
to shake out the beach sand

and at your foot
tiny
my God, what a foot that was
I remember
how you fought with the waiter
when he brought me the wrong drink
not the one I'd ordered
how we made love
with the TV on
a romantic movie blaring
I teach you my tongue
by rolling poetry off it
I see you
sitting on the edge of the bath
while I am shaving
you are massaging in face cream
the hydrating make-up base
whatever
I see you collecting dry leaves around the garden
only the beautiful ones;
they still fall out
from books long left unopened
I remember
when you went to another room
to make secret phone calls
I pretended to read the paper
the financial reports
God forgive me, I was so…
I remember
your dog
our puppy, rather
who came up to the bed every morning
and burrowed between us
I remember
The first time you left
I looked out of the window
into an empty street
into the night
there was a poster for a cowboy movie
across the road
the radiators were cold
the boiler in the bathroom

Serbia

hissed
and
your eyes
were there as soon as I closed mine
I remember
the smell of your clothes
forgotten in the cupboard
a large cardboard box
full of photos
God, what did I do with them?
Which one of my houses moves
was the end of them?
I remember
quiet evenings
you painting
and me writing
or reading in the armchair
I remember
The flowers which kept arriving
each morning
suffusing the apartment
with their oppressive smell
perhaps I should have asked
who was sending them
perhaps
I remember the night sounds
your breathing
and the muffled song of the drunks
coming from below
I remember how,
when you were to go "somewhere",
I hurried you along
so you wouldn't be late
pretending to have no clue
and how you came back
from hospital alone
with blue
black
rings around your eyes
something needed saying
I know
As soon as I was away

you packed your suitcases
bags
toiletry bags
some of the things even spilled over
into the woven basket for the market
I remember
your silence in answer to my question
I remember
my silence in answer to your silence
I remember gazing through the window
and the sound of your key on the kitchen table
and the sound of the apartment door, opening
I remember
hitting you on the face
(All my life, my hand will follow
That trajectory)
and I remember you crying
well before impact

Serbia

Jasmina Topić (1977, Pancevo, Serbia) writes poetry, short prose, essays, and columns. She has fewest co-authored prose publications and six sole-authored poetry books: "Suncokreti. Skica za dan" / Sunflowers. Portrait for the day (1997), "Pansion. Metamorfoze" / Pension. Methamorphoses (2001), "Romantizam" / Romanticism (2005), "Tiha obnova leta" / The Quiet Renewal of the Summer (2007), "Dok neko šapuće naša imena" / While Someone is Whispering Our Names (2012) and "Plaža Nesanica" / Beach Insomnia (2016). Most of her books were short-listed for eminent poetry prizes in her home country, and she is included in several representative anthologies, the latest is "Cat Painters" - Contemporary Serbian poetry from Second World War until today, published by Dialogos, New Orleans, USA (2017). She is an Editor in chief since 1998 of Rukopisi / Manuscripts - a collection of poetry and short prose of young authors from former Yugoslavia, published by Youth Center from Pančevo, Serbia; and also a co-editor of contemporary poetry edition "The Best One", published by Society of writers and literary translators Pančevo. Jasmina Topic's poetry is translated into several European languages and she was participating in some outstanding poetry festivals in the Balkan region and beyond. Also, she had a couple of important European scholarships aka Artist in residence programs: Kultur Kontakt, Vienna, Austria (2008), Kamov Residency, Rijeka, Croatia (2012), Poeteca, Tirana, Albania (2013), RONDO, Graz, Austria (2014) and Create in Residence, BCWT (Baltic centre for writers and translators) Visby, Gotland, Sweden (2014). She is a member of Serbian Literary Society.

We Never Lived Except When Reading

I got lost in the space of a book,
the words of a poem in an unknown language followed me,
warm Mediterranean ethnic music, like joint
stays on islands where joy is always to be renewed.

Two spaces edged by shadows and music
annulled me; they brought me down to the level
of a line not drawn,
at the bottom of a sheet, outside the footnote.

Where belonging was dying out
the passion for writing emerged, for one
of the possible worlds washed out by salt
like a misprint.

And the space of the book changed our facial
form, gave us a purpose. And I was. –
Truly attached to verses, to pictures
the way I was to a shoulder of bygone times,
dreaming of northern seas so lively,
from those letters arranged into verses.

I listened, waiting for gold bugs
to start milling across my skin, trembling. I resided
under polar light, within arm's reach of the otherness
of another, real life...

But we never lived except when reading, sizing up
that which preceded and followed the writing while your eyes,
tiny nutshells on the line of the imaginary,
were both the sea and insomnia.

Now I slide slowly by the glacier whose names
and purpose I do not recognise.
And as if in a deep, deepest dream under ice floes,
occasional voices call out to me from the light
in which it is no longer possible to reside.
This morning, from dawn till dusk.

Lodgers

We were quiet. Just like those tiny skinny birds
unaware of this world.

We are still morose.

My body always dehydrates slightly next to yours.
Your body is soft and I squeeze
from it the holy water of my shortcomings.
The water that I always lack.
Soap bubbles and detergent bubbles,
two products from the same department, that's
what we achieved straining to attain the ideal.

We fly around this flat like the feathers
of plucked pigeons ready to be made into a good soup.

Everyone sitting at his or her computer,
achieves his or her objectives in video games. I've reached the next level.
We are negotiating on Second life.

The loser gets to take broken fragments
to the great city dump.

I know that when all's said and done we'll become even quieter.
The dent in the bed grows like any suburb.

We did not move into that flat.
It's getting warmer and summer will be upon us soon.

Translation from Serbian into English by Novica Petrović

She Does Not. She Is No Ofelia

She opens the windows and closes her eye-lids,
The day is in a perfect winterly peace
and no sound can disturb the pause between two emptiness:
The one she finds herself in and the one
she is about to lay down in.

Beneath the eye-lids a restless pupil is boiling
its desire to look, always to see, just one more time,
a possible path. It trembles without peace like a bird's wing,
a nervous twitter on the clear blue,

it won't look ahead
it won't fall asleep

She is awake under the low sky of a ceiling,
but her body does not want to move into the outside world.
The world is a playground wired with the edge of the bed,
And behind the eye-lids, the lids are melting in drops,
a spleen of inner maps, of a differently described city:

it won't look ahead
it won't fall asleep

The first haze is over, the warm body has gone by,
A summer slipped like a sand, out of nowhere between her teeth,
Crushed in the future quarry -
She sings a quiet song, she is quiet, nothing can get to her,
not a single voice of reason, no one can touch her anymore

it won't look ahead
it won't fall asleep

She closes her eyes reaching for a newly discovered darkness
She comes, she stays, she is giving up
And continuously melting in drops when in contact
with the fresh air.

Translation from Serbian into English by Lara Jakica and the author

Serbia

Zvonko Karanović used to worked as a journalist, radio host, DJ, concert organizer, and he was the owner of a music store for thirteen years. He was starting to write draw on Beat literature, film, and pop culture. He experiments with surrealism and form of prose poems in his latest work phase.

Until now, he published nine collections of poems and three novels. His poems have been translated to sixteen languages and published in several international editions, all representative literary magazines in South-Eastern Europe, as well as numerous both Serbian and international anthologies (most significant *New European Poets,* Graywolf Press, USA, Minnesota, 2008). He received several Serbian literary awards for poetry and many international fellowships for writers (such as "Heinrich Boll Foundation" fellowship, Cologne, Germany, 2011).

Karanović is a member of Serbian PEN. Lives and works in Belgrade.

The Gentle Crush of Lines around the Lips

on the dark streets
there's no one to see the dash through puberty
the gentle crush of lines around the lips
each smile lasts
twelve days
each small sun
disappears into the sugar box
the scars are fields of roses
on Prom's dreamy skin
and for all that,
the South is still wild
anesthetized with guilt
the paper sky of the industrial town
burns with an unforgettable fire
and mythic images of
the senseless slaughterhouse of dreams
resemble a bloody liver in the dirt
my new shelter is called TV
while I embrace the past
the stereo bears witness
and I admit
I always felt like Jesus' son
searching for lost luxury
I asked once
where does breakfast sleep
once I made love with a sumo beauty
once I found comfort on a great wave of confetti
once I slowly, slowly like a moron
unwrapped the pack of Marlboros
lit up
and blew smoke into the spring day

Bikini for Baby, Blues for the Dewdrop

the woman held the child in her arms
in front of the cardboard barracks
on whose wall
the graffiti read
CHARLIE GONNA BE A NAPALM STAR!
I thought the world was
a bucket of dirty laundry
that a great fiery ball
will forever merge with silence
and then I hit the gas
a moment later
everything turned to oblivion

last night I dreamed
they stole all my sweaters
and set them on fire
and I was cold
terribly cold under the crown
of the old plane tree that shed its bark
at the feet of chance passers-by
when I woke
I found this note:
you're a nervous urban wreck
buried in pop culture trash

art is something you can run away with
but it's just a daytrip from which
you must return
with ironed faces
the strong and mighty mimes
smirked from the election posters
as a reminder that life
never loses to amateurs
politics has a fake aura of innocence
only the marathon is
a triumph of spirit over matter

just like at every first snow
I bummed around the downtown
and watched the snowflakes
cover the drabness of
socialist architecture
raised my hands
and turned the palms up to the sky
so they'd remember the dance
of those white defenseless princesses

Burn, Baby, Burn!

no one wants to buy
my perfect face
the smooth pages of foreign magazines
I collected and kept
to light a fire
when snow
buries the windows
my eyes are called boredom
on the streets, cold this summer
my mother is a feature film
I'll forget
as soon as I close the door
I need
attention
just like artists
kids and criminals
your thick eyebrows
your bare feet
the birthmark above your upper lip
oh, Cindy
you're just a wild desire
from that street where it never snows
fidelity is an essence
that can't be attained
memories are not enough
for the years of futile struggle
except for Cinderella carried by the current
in her chrome casket
I sliced my skin with a razor
because it rushes into old age
and leaves me
in this
youth
that won't pass

Translated by Ana Božičević

Sofija Živković (1985), graduated in Serbian philology from the Faculty of Philology, Belgrade. Published two books of poetry Sobe (Rooms) and Kafa u pet (Coffe at Five), a book of creative nonfiction Intimni vodič kroz Dorćol i okolinu (An Intimate Guide through Dorćol and surroundings) and a book of selected poems in Serbian, German and Hungarian Trojna monarhija. She reguary publishes poems and essays in acclaimed magazines in Serbia and some of them have been translated into Arabic, Albanian, Spanish. Her poems were incuded in a regiona female poetry anthology Ovo nije dom (This is not home) and her short story (translated into German) was included in a fiction anthology about Vienna's Danube shore entitled Zu anderen Unfern, which will come out during 2018 in Vienna. She was guest of the art festival Sommerloch in Vienna 2016 and will be translator-in-residence (translating from Spanish) at the Europaische Ubersetzung Kollegium in Germany in August 2018. She is preparing a new book of peetry based on painting of Berliner painter Lesser Ury.

Gundulićev Venac Street

I see the façade of the building that belongs there,
Beyond border,
As in that street another time is worth and
There's no cold as here where I am;
While I burn a cigarette, Kent, on terrace there's a snow,
sowed pine tree
And the butt with the lipstick imprint; I love
The smell of tobacco while it mixes with the sound
Of cigarette afterburning, and after all – after some memories
And a nicotine taste, ashes remain, which I casually shake
On terrace, I throw the butt and
I lock the room door.
I count that langsyne
That impossible
That lancinating absence on snows,
Here near the Die lange Gasse;
and when I wake up tomorrow,
And the air freshened by the frozen river,
 again I'm going to go,
There beyond the border.
Yet this sole cigarette, this time - only.

Broken Jewelry

Let's open a jeweler shop
That has only the broken jewelry
With broken pitchers and vases
Noggins and jewelry again
On what did this recalls you?
 Someone was touching another
With jewelry in fingers
Around the neck and in a heart
With brooch in the heart
As you did to me
Sometimes
Always
Timelessly
Out of any expectation
Yet in a long waiting

Nocturno

You can not say
What you hear
It is just as you go in the street
We stop around the corner
29th November- Cetinjska street and
There's no signboard
There's no even a path
Only no
No we do not want to go
With clamminess life has been painted
You can't erase
Nor restore
Light through windows pierces
The windows are unreal
But they made us transparent
As somebody plays a tune
There in your room
But there's no room
As if somebody plays Glass' etude 5
But there's no piano
There's no Pianist
Return us
Bring us back in the same point
To hear again
Again to hear that same all .

Poems from the collection KAFA U PET (COFFE AT FIVE), translation: Fahredin Shehu

BILALL MALIQI is a writer, poet and publicist, was born in on 08.04.1969 in a village Elez Bali, municipality of Presheva. He writes poetry and prose for children and adults, he deals also with literature critics. He is the author of 28 works: poetry for children, for adults, prose for children and adults, journalism and literary critics. Anthologies: the magazine Panorama by the authors of South East Kosova " Sigh for Earth " by the author Hysen Keqiku (2004) ; In lexicon " authors of Albanian Literature for children and adults 1886- 2009" by prof. as.dr. Astrit Bishqemi; in poetical antology Albanian- Swedish "Fllamande Ballad" by Sokol Demaku (2009); In poetical anthology "The Echo of Centuries"by Sokol Demaku, (2010). In International Poetical Anthology "Open Lane "by Kristaq Shabani (2012); In poetical anthology by dr. Fatmir Terziu " Virgin Tears, (2012); In Belgium Poetical Anthology French-Albanian " Anthologie de poetes Albanophones(2012); Maliqi is a founder and editor in chief of the magazine "Qendresa" which is published in Presheva Valley. Maliqi is a president of association of Presheva writers; Maliqi is a member of League of Writers of Kosova; Member of the board " Atunis" President of "Atunis Lugina" in Presheva.

Open Your Eyes

Open your eyes
I get into groan

Close your eyes
A black shadow
Around us

Open your files
And take off your masks

Because the fortress of Presheva
Is covered by darkness
Whereas the Valley is covered by dread

Open your eyes…

Longing For Fate

Fortune of mine only you know my pains
I revealed and had inside me

When sleepy loneliness overtakes me
The memory is linked strongly with longing

My longing is stretched in belly of time
For the moisture fate in the edge of soul

I never give up to annoyance
Neither to storm that takes a bunch of memories

My saturated fate in a pond of tears
My hope left in a dirty midnight

My desire for you as the wide fields
From where came the first word of love

My song for you was transformed into a ballade
Together with damned landmarks

Upon our sights fell out darkness
And put us into legend

Now in the nest of ruined fate
Remained a hope which will never disappear

Patching My Ramshackle Fate

Let me patch my ramshackle fate
In the back of the contempt map

Let me count the shouts
And with my look to destroy the landmark

Let me step down the slope
With many repeated groan

Let me sit on the top of the landmark
And get connected with you my land

Let me be on the surface of the rocky ground
Just to read the engraved love

The Grandeur lays in a basin of one's Pain,
Perseverance, and ability to Forgive

Slovenia

Maja Vidmar was born in 1961. She comes from Nova Gorica and lives in Ljubljana as a free-lance poet. Her first book *Distances of the Body - Razdalje telesa* (1984) was sold in 1500 copies and it drew a lot of attention, among other things because of its erotic theme, Until present she has published seven collections of poems: besides the first one also *Ways of Binding - Način vezave*, 1988; *At the Base - Ob vznožju*, 1998; *Presence - Prisotnost*, 2005; *Rooms - Sobe*, 2008; *How to Fall in Love - Kako se zaljubiš*, 2012 and *Minutes of Advantage - Minute prednosti,* 2015, as well as two books of collected poems *Urge of Direction - Ihta smeri smeri*, 1989 and *Fifty Poems - Petdeset pesmi*, 2015. Using a concise and ever simpler language in her poems she gives poetic expression to what she is a part of, and above all what is part of her. In the last years this has been organically complemented by her interest and involvement in gestalt therapy which serves her as the guiding principle in creating poetry writting workshops which she leads. Her book *Prisotnost* was awarded the Jenko prize, the prize Nagrada Prešernovega sklada and brought her the Wienna scholarship of Grosser Preis für osteuropäische Literatur. She was awarded Premio Letterario Internazionale Trieste Scriture di Frontiera dedicato a Umberto Saba 2007, and for the book *Sobe* the prize Nagrada mreže gradova književnosti 2009. For her poetry in the last ten years she was awarded the prize Velenjica – the Cup of Immortality 2015. Her poetry is widely translated in other languages and seven books of her poetry were published in other languages: *Leibhaftige Gedichte* (Droschel, 1999), for which she was awarded the prize Hubert-Burda-Stifung für junge Lyrik, *Akt* (Meandar, 1999), *Molitva tijela* (Tugra, 2007), *Gegenwart* (Edition Korrespondenzen, 2007), *Način vezivanja* (Udruženje književnika Banja Luka, 2009), *E il mondo si scolora* (Ibiskos Editore, 2010) and *Izby a ine basne* (Studna 2015). She has many poems published in Slovene and foreign literary reviews and anthologies.

The Drumroll Rehearsal

Silently imagine
a symphonic orchestra
among the trees in the middle
of a forest. Think of a brown cello
stuck in the soft ground, the drums
scattered here and there, and the smooth
chopping block of the timpani.
Replace the golden edging
of the black tree trunks for the luster
of the stretched trombone
and do not overlook the shiver
of the violin bows alongside
the oak shoots. Be a robin
fluttering off onto a thin branch
of the flute, and a flutist
holding her breath.
Then breathe through all
the possible swaps,
replace the skins along with
the black varnish of the soil, and hope
for the silence of the crack.

Luck

Most of my problems
have to do with luck. It
swaggers about my house,
shifting my objects,
especially the paperweights,
every day it acts out
an earthquake and the end
of the world, so now I
understand why some
people, when luck knocks
on their door, prefer to get
sick, close the shutters,
and die.

With luck,
it's either luck or the house.
It wouldn't let me keep
anything else either.
The sorrowful pillar of salt
I've hardly scratched
from earth doesn't exist.
Tiredness, not at all!
Incompetence,
what's that?

Luckily, I don't care
for the house or the
paperweights, not even
sorrow as much as it may
seem at times. I find it hard
to part with tiredness, with
incompetence, but
everything would still be
pretty much okay if only
I knew who now carries
my name and who now
enters and exits where
there is no house.

Slovenia

Is it possible for me to
be sold by accident
at some market? Could it
happen that my own
mother wouldn't
recognize me, just
offering me some tea
in surprise, sending me
away, with me thinking
she's right?

(How You Fall in Love, 2012)

Peter Semolič, born in Ljubljana in 1967, studied General Linguistics and Cultural Studies at the University of Ljubljana. He is the author of fourteen books of poetry: *Tamarisk* (1991), *The Roses of Byzantium* (1994), *House Made of Words* (1996), *Circles Upon the Water* (2000), *Questions About the Path* (2001), *Border* (2002) *The Bog Fires* (2004), *A place for You* (2006), *The Journey Around the Sun* (2008), *The Milky Way* (2009), *Poems and Letters* (2009), *Night in the Middle of the Day* (2012), *The Other Shore* (2015) and *Obiski / Visite* (Visits – bilingual Slovenian-Italian book) (2015). He has received many prizes for his work, including, *Jenko's Poetry Prize* (1997), *Prešeren Prize* (the National Award for Literature and Arts), 2001 and *Časa nesmrtnosti* (2016). In 1998 he also won the *Vilenica Crystal Award*. Peter Semolič also writes plays, children's literature, essays and translates from English, French, Serbian and Croatian. He is co-founder and co-editor of the first Slovenian online poetry magazine Poiesis (http://www.poiesis.si/).

The Navje Cemetery*

So let's step inside, step into the sacred space, among the golden
corpses, as the early spring
sun already sparkles on the light green leaves
and leaks into the greyness of the old tombstones… More real
in their books, even in school textbooks, then here,
they are still so much themselves, free of grammatical rules,
whispering in the language of early grass, the sizzling of candles,
the hum of the breeze that blows along the path we
walk on; they are themselves more than ever before.
We stop by the arch vestibule, where an angel spreads
his scorched wings above one of the tombs. Or has
somebody sprayed them black? We don't pray
for their escaped souls, we don't honour their
merits for the nation. We keep silent. We listen to the blackbird singing
in the nearby bush, and another one responding from behind
the wall that divides the world of the dead from the world of the living.
A cloud blocks the sun… or perhaps it's suddenly evening…

*Navje is a memorial park in Ljubljana, with tombstones of personalities who played a significant part in Slovenian history.

Translated by Barbara Jurša

An Icy Rain

Blessed are gods for their immortality?
I heard Achilles' horses cry over Patroclus,
I saw the bloody rock with which Cain
killed Abel, my father and my brother –
they lied, turned into a stone, serene
as two gigantic pebbles on a riverbank.
An icy rain above Ljubljana and my face is already
pricked to the point of bleeding, tears from the wind in my eyes.
A language without tropes, a black-and-white drawing on paper
spanning even beyond the horizon, an infinite
repetition in mirrors placed opposite each
other – they will never die, that's for sure,
but if something doesn't die, has it ever lived at all?
The morning coffee is pleasantly warm and the girl who
walks by – and I've told myself not to write
about this anymore! – is truly beautiful: a red parka
on the background of snow melting more and more, disappearing.

Translated by Barbara Jurša

Colors

Your eyes are blue, blue is your color.
Near the evening, the yellow forsythia flowers and a full
moon above the apartment blocks close by – you have made a
step and I, though still brown, walk by your side,
suddenly no longer staggering, your step
is thirty-two years long and smells like an orange.
I haven't expected it, not even in a dream – tonight we
shared in it white bread and then called forth,
no longer in a dream, big red
blossoms to our faces. Which colour is your favourite one?
Which male singer? Which female one? Summertime sadness
is behind us and the black voice of Lana del Rey is no longer a sign,
but just another song like any other.
Light green grass, dark green in the moonlight,
you, who don't believe in yourself yet, I, who have believed in you
from the moment you came with rosemary and mint,
believe in us. The color of your eyes changes
with light, at night they shine with their own – two stars,
no longer shrouded by any cloud of dark matter.

Translated by Barbara Jurša

Poetry from the Balkans

Andrej Blatnik (1963, Ljubljana, Slovenia) studied Comparative Literature and Sociology of Culture and got his PhD in Communication Studies. He is an Associate Professor of Publishing Studies at the University of Ljubljana, edits a book series of 'modern classics' in one of Slovenian major publishing houses and was the president of the jury for the Vilenica Central European Literary Prize between 2008 and 2015.

He has published three novels, five collections of short stories, three books of cultural studies and a 'how-to' book on short story writing. He translated several books from English, including Sylvia Plath's *The Bell Jar* and *The Sheltering Sky* by Paul Bowles.
Andrej Blatnik won some major literary awards (the award of the city of Ljubljana, Zlata ptica, the highest award for young artists, the Slovenian national state award, Prešeren Fund, and the Russian best Slavic book of short fiction 'Jugra' award in 2016 among them).

Andrej Blatnik has read fiction around the globe, on literary festivals such as PEN World Voices in New York City, Toronto International Festival of Authors, Jaipur Literary Festival and Cosmopolis in Barcelona, was a participant of the International Writing Program at the University of Iowa, Iowa City, USA, in 1993, and a guest at the International Writers Center at the Old Dominion University, Norfolk, Virginia, USA, in 1995. He received various fellowships, including Fulbright. A list of his publications, along with some samples, is available at www.andrejblatnik.com.

Garage
for Karl Browski

Dear God, I hope you don't mind that we don't call on you as often as you'd want. We have our hands full. Lots of work.

Dear God, thank you for granting our wishes and getting rid of the new guy for us. There was no other way. Straight off he started talking about pay and conditions, disrupting our lunch breaks; discussions like that just start fights, everyone knows who works and who distributes the money, each to his own, that's the way of the world, who are we to change that? This guy, he wanted to turn us into martyrs, and we don't want that, we want to live and work!

You must understand, we were glad when the boss bashed his face in with a crowbar, and no, it wasn't just because we were worried about our paychecks that we told the police we didn't know what went down, that accidents happen in our line of work. It was better that way, dear God. We had to wash the floor, but now we're happy we can go on working; it was getting unbearable, now our garage is peaceful again.

Astral Separation

Tired out by the tediousness of the day, the couple by the pool eagerly read to each other what their horoscopes promise. What wonderful things are forecast! Long-lasting love, loads of money, good kids. This is one good vacation, they think, we've chosen well, but that's to be expected, we're good people, the world is just.

But lo and behold, trouble is looming; the heavens must have played a dirty trick, or else the astrologer has cheated, slapping together an astral prediction after a night on the booze without consulting the stars, because their real, adverse fate isn't written anywhere: A few minutes from now, one of the gardeners pruning a bush by the pool with an electric trimmer will slip so unfortunately he'll end up in the water, trimmer and all. In the water where right now they're playfully splashing each other and thinking about what to name the baby they may have conceived yesterday.

Electricity and water, that can't end well. Screams, ambulance sirens, but nothing to be done. Then come the banner headlines, speculations about negligence and malpractice, wonderings as to whether such trimmers shouldn't have been disused long ago, cancellations of reservations, and in a few months' time the hotel will have to close, the whole thing won't blow over as the owners will hope.

No one will ever know that it wasn't the astrologer's fault, that he had drawn up his prognoses as painstakingly as always, that something had gone wrong in the heavens, had gone against expectations. There will be no children and no prosperity. The heavens are sometimes so messy.

Slovenia

We're Not

It was okay when I managed to sleep. But when I couldn't, I'd think about you and our future. I knew it wouldn't last. Sure, we'd soon sleep together. But what would that change? We're not a good match, we both know that, together and apart. And yet I went for all those coffees with you, coffees that had long ceased being just coffees, and all those drinks, who could remember what they were. And we knew every time that we're not. And yet you asked me out over and over again, and over and over again I said maybe, okay, let's, I never said that we're not. Maybe I should've said it the moment I knew it; but I knew it straight away and then there would've been no coffees, no drinks, no invitations. Then I should've told myself: I'm not. That sounds so lonesome. We're not is better, much better.

Poetry from the Balkans

Ivo Frbéžar, Mala Ilova Gora, Slovenia; Poet, writer, editor, ilustrator, publisher (Publishing House MONDENA, Grosuplje, Slovenia /EU), graphic designer, photographer...

Living in small village Mala Ilova Gora in Slovenia. Work like an independent writer/poet. Studied Comparative literature and literary theory on Filozofska fakulteta in Ljubljana (Faculty of Art in Ljubljana), and LSPR (London School of Public Relation.

Member of DSP, Društvo slovenskih pisateljev (Assosiation of Slovenian Writers) and Slovenskega centra PEN (Slovenian PEN Centre; Member of board, ex. Vice President), member of his Translaters&Lingvistic Rights Commitee (T&LRC) and IABC (Addvertising&Business Communications)
.
Writing poetry, short stories, radiodrama. Ilustrate books and covers. Published 15 books of poetry, short stories, haiku, aforism, 2 abroad (Czechia and Macedonia, several book in preparing: Bulgaria, Serbia, Croatia, Italy. Translation in english, italian, macedonian, bulgarian, polish, serbo-croatian languages avaliable. Published in several Literary Magazines in Slovenia and abroad. Radioplay translated in english in slovak Language, published in english (Slovenian radio drama) and represented on EBU Contest and Slovak National Radio.

Awarded by some International Prices for poetry and graphic design.

Crucified

She abandoned the shores of Anatolia
Of ancient Halicarnassus, and the memories
Of the mausoleum of one of the Seven Wonders of the World
Sailed around the little island and landed on the Island of Kos
She saw the remains of the Temple of Asclepius
The Kos once adorned by marble statues
With massive crowds of the sick
On a pilgrimage to their god,
Hoping to relieve their pain
Asclepius came to them in their dreams and healed them
Healed the dead brought dead lovers back to life
Unborn children he revived and trusted them to Centaur
He broke the law so Zeus hit him with his lightning
Apollo saving him from his punishment
Was Asclepius a god or a healer
Who healed the sick with incubation in their dreams
I woke up in the mausoleum
A young and hungry woman
I shall pay for yielding to temptation
For my wildly beating heart
I know about the blood, blood, about the womb
The womb is like fertile soil
I know and the jet budding from it is poetry
I know the scarlet streaming forth again and again
Through the pores from sweet and deep throats of vaginal
Blooming miracles do happen
I no longer recognize myself I am a lake
A river luring you to plunge into me and let your breath out
I shall look for a new shore if necessary
I fall in love recklessly and juggle with
My double who believes in ghosts
And not in destiny not in love
Not in art not in the rhythm of the heart
Poor cripple unaware of her limp
And what is worst she doesn't even bother
She is never satisfied
Doesn't believe in dreams

I make love every night
Stupefied I cry in pure lust and so what
I know Dostoevsky said the future
Antichrist will tempt us with beauty
dream a peaceful dream my dearest creature she says to me
let us go back to the land of childhood she says to me
we'll look like other people there
we'll find the place that will make us happy
though my vagina and my legs bleed
step by step hug by hug
some of us women are stretched like a cross
spread open and waiting to be
touched ...

translated by Janko Lozar

Slovenia

I will speak more and more softly
from Collection Orosilo / Bedewed

I will speak more and more softly
until my words are whispered
like those of sinner
in the confessional

I will whisper more and more softly
until I susurrate
like leaves
in the wind

I will susurrate more and more softly
until my voice resembles
the voice of the sand
by the sea

and only those
who linger
and listen
will hear me

translated by Herbert Kuhner and Feliks J. Bister

Anti / SONETS

52.

I never sleep I live and dream and I dream when
I live and when I sleep that's living as well said
Fernando Pessoa we are only what we dream
And don't see what we see but only

What we are Mr. Krakar too had determined the world
He had observed from his skyscraper almost everyone
He equally hated to some extent he felt alone
In his own dreams there was not much human left

In it he become a mischievous old man that waits for
A gust of wind to tip him memories he'd like to write
But even his dreams he doesn't remember likewise titles

Have faded do not laugh at my forgetfulness
He begged converse with me so that I will remember
Who I am and that I'm not somewhere else

Slovenia

Primož Čučnik was born in Ljubljana in 1971. He studied philosophy and sociology of culture at the University of Ljubljana. His first collection of poetry, Dve Zimi (Two Winters), was published in 1999 and received the Best First Collection Award. His latest books are Delo in dom (Work and Home, 2008), Kot dar (As a Gift, 2010), Mikado (2012), Trilogija (Trilogy, Selected poems, 2015) in Ti na s (You with D, 2017). His poems were anthologized in A Fine Line: New Poetry from Eastern & Central Europe. He translates contemporary Polish and American poetry. He has published (co)translations of works by Adam

Wiedemann, Marcin Świetlicki, Piotr Sommer, Eugenyusz Tkaczyszyn Dycki and Miron Białoszewski as well as Frank O'Hara, Elizabeth Bishop and John Ashbury. He also writes literary criticism, essays and works as an editor of the magazine Literatura, and runs the small press Sherpa.

Pastoral Hide And Seek

We left the city and ploughed into a fog
descending like creeping irony.
We rushed through a tunnel and the fog dispersed into sun dust.
It drew a rainbow on the windshield.

The cause was a gray curtain of rain from ages ago
mixed with a crystal blue river of sky, and waves
of clouds foaming. The cause was a delicate
game of echoes and shadows, branches rocking in errands of wind.

January sun and September rain at once,
we never experienced that before! Eighty
miles per hour we drove through the open door
of afternoon, promising magnificent returns.

Almost priceless. And almost blessed.
A fatigue produced by our walk
through the vineyard hills, and the view;
rested on green brown rugs of the valley,

in the steep bell tower strikes the hour like a whisper
in an unimagined distance. It was familiar to us.
Once we already bowed down to its quiet, whining
sighs. We could try something else this time.

Perhaps going deeper into the woods, where we've never been
and getting lost on marked trails. Perhaps
listening to some unfamiliar bird which will sing
just after the cuckoo. Perhaps repeating the same song

but in a new way, before the leas grow dark
and we won't find a way back, in darkness
waiting for the day – to shine on us again
with mild dew on blueberry bushes and skin.

Slovenia

These are the areas where an axe didn't chop yet
to cleave the trunks and leave those stump impressions.
That was clear. But we might feel embarrassed
in front of the spruce tree's nakedness or our naked fingers.

Therefore we watched ourselves from a clever distance
and just whispering in an ear, into a mouthpiece of whistle.
Once it was the hands of a shepherd and now
it's lying on the ground, waiting for its happy finder.

We asked him to give it back and name it
like the climbing direction which he climbed
in his elastic climbing shoes. To rename it.
Together we could catch jerky movements of shadows and sun.

Then we saw the city again, in the middle of the afternoon,
in a moment when the dust of the new morning had just ascended.
The clouds, squeezed and twisted, made way for azure reflection.
And the fog is sadly looking around for errands of wind.

Bad Weather

There's no explanation for what's
happening in tiny drops for the third day now.
And no prediction. Those long term
ones are wrong, but the short ones are late,
talking about things we already know.

I don't know why, but that's how we talk.
We'll never get used to permanent
changes and changeability, otherwise
we would talk differently. If there's
a world that's different, we'll manage.

But we'll never find out,
as we know, only through intuition.
With its satin touch. If there's
a world like that, we'll
actually manage. Without lies and threats.

Well. I'd like to give you a present
I was saving for you, but I don't know
if I'm going out or even if you'll be invited
over, in the form of salty drops
or questions.

Old Toys

A few echoes, just a hair
too loud, come out of doubt,
daydream into expanding universe
built from dust and oars.

Roots fly in wisps
behind the uprooted trunks,
like launched rockets
with radiant tails.

Boats full of weightlessness
are rocking on masses –
on creamy clouds
beneath refined wings.

In the most neglected flight
the body draws a loop
that tied with a smile
might burst above this town.

We play about
in what cannot be said,
strangers in some future solitude
that can hardly wait to smile at you –

to avenge itself on you
that love – shy, spontaneous, inviting.

Translated from Slovene by Ana Pepelnik and Joshua Beckma

Forgiveness is a release
from somebody else's burden of hatred

Turkey

Tarık Günersel

Poet, playright, actor and director, Tarık Günersel worked at Istanbul City Theater as a dramaturg. His works include *Breaths of Infinity* (Sonsuzluk Solukları, a mosaic of poems), and *My 300th Birthday Speech* (short stories). *Becoming* (Oluşmak) consists of is a collection of his aphorisms and various ideas from world wisdom. His plays include *Billennium, Nero and Agrippina, Sociology of Shit, Threat*, and *Virtually Yours*. He has written four libretti for the composer Selman Ada: *Ali Baba & 40, Blue Dot, Forbidden Love, and Another Planet*. His translations into Turkish include works by Arthur Miller, Samuel Beckett, Vaclav Havel ad Savyon Liebrecht. His presentation of World Poetry Day to PEN International in 1997 led to its adoption by UNESCO. Ex-president of PEN Turkey Center, in Tokyo he was elected to PEN International Board for 2010-12. In 2013 he initiated the Earth Civilization Project with various intellectuals from around the world.

Europe is Dying in Bosnia

Europe is watching herself being tortured,
raped and killed.
Long live, Barbarity! You are almighty.
The future, too, is yours.
Long live, Barbarity! The future will also
be your obedient servant
       like today's angels of "free" enterprise or state
       like today's workers of the world
       like today's believers and non-believers.
We are your obedient servants, Barbarity.
You are the ruler of the world.
Thank us: Thanks to us.

Forgive us, children
                -born or yet to be born
Forgive us Jesus, forgive us Marx
Forgive us Bruno, Mother Teresa, Mme Curie
Forgive us the Unknown Resistance Fighter
Forgive us, all those who lived for human
liberation and peace
Forgive us, children
For we cannot forgive ourselves.

Forgive us, those who've been tortured and killed
Forgive us, those who're being tortured and killed
Forgive us, those who will be tortured and killed

Hitler rests in peace.
Europe is dying in Bosnia.
The rest is… "easy". More and more.

1994

Poetry from the Balkans

9/!!

!! !!
!! !!
!! !!
!! !!
!! !!
!! !!
!! !!
!! !!
!! !!
!! !!
!! !!
!! !!
!! !!
!! !!
!! !!
!! !!
!! !!
!! !!
!! !!
!! !!
!! !!
!! !!
!! !!
!! !!
!! !!
!! !!
!! !!
!! !!
!! !!
!! !!
!! !!
!! !!
!! !!
!! !!
!! !!
!! !!

Newer York

Turkey

"Life"

image storms, stormy images, storm images

          image factories
          image operations, autopsies

          solution images
   desires for desire image
          image wars, captives
                victories of victory image
       image image
          image of image image
   victory of the image of image image,
      image of victory image of image image

      image of images
              image of supreme
  competitions of supreme images
       competition of competitions of supreme image

    friendship image, image friendship
              frienship to friendship image

    image of seeking truth

   image particles
         memories

    cemetery of images

   cemetery of images of cemetery of images

He was born in Istanbul (1979) and lives in there. He works in a logistics company. His publications include poems, stories and essays. His works were published in Karabatak, Karagöz and Ücra such are national journals in Turkey. His first poem book named "İlk Değilim Üstelik" was published in 2014 and second poem book named "Kuş Adımı" was published in 2016.

Winter Fear

snowing with your eyes
in this century
a huge winter is coming down
with your hands
it is obvious that it will not be over just with snow but
freezing hail in jar
with the sound of snow
will grow up in spring

I told a mistake
Not by mistake
What I told was not a mistake
I told a mistake
done and
repeated everyday
Because they left the garden
with a mistake
that took us to winter

then: penitence

it is possible to survive from winter through mercy
new yards were constructed under the shadow of a mercy
it is possible to enter into the gardens
that we wait for with a mercy
it should be done in winter
maybe it is better
to join the ones
who left the garden first with a mercy

Kids expecting fun are behind the windows
frozen pictures of the future days
it was a winter with full of frightening nights
getting darker and darker
they were looking at the moon
far away in their dreams
kids are behind
the windows with their eyes on the ice.

middle section: beautification

kept in winter
snow bestowed from the sky
may kill and recreate
as it rains,
water will leak in existence
beneficence
leaving a deep breath
in vessels.
Hung steam,
winter will come in this garden too
birds should shelter or migrate
but gardens are far away
deep breath
unless he kills the seed in this garden
and buries it in solid sand
and makes it green again
we can't know to
which home this derelict old home
or a mansion opens
if he doesn't make the seed green again
wouldn't we wither away

more: fear

prosperous freshness of penalties
from winter is postponed to winter
even though it was grown up in summer
thanks god we saw sorrow in winter
if we spend the winter in this way
what a pity the summer ends
the summer will be over and again winter
we will die and be born
we will die and be born
and again winter
snow.

Translated by Mehmet ASMALI and Ufuk CELIK

This Anthological Publication is underwritten solely by

Inner Child Press International

Inner Child Press International is a Publishing Company Founded and Operated by Writers. Our personal publishing experiences provides us an intimate understanding of the sometimes-daunting challenges Writers, New and Seasoned may face in the Business of Publishing and Marketing their Creative "Written Work".

For more Information

Inner Child Press International

intouch@innerchildpress.com
www.innerchildpress.com